CAROLINE CLIFTON-MOGG

Summers
IN FRANCE

BEAUTIFUL &
INSPIRATIONAL
FRENCH HOMES

RYLAND PETERS & SMALL
LONDON • NEW YORK

W0009101

Senior designer Megan Smith
Editor Sophie Devlin
Picture research Jess Walton
Senior commissioning editor Annabel Morgan
Head of production Patricia Harrington
Creative director Leslie Harrington

First published in 2023 by
Ryland Peters & Small
20–21 Jockey's Fields,
London WC1R 4BW
and
341 East 116th Street
New York, NY 10029

www.rylandpeters.com

Text copyright © Caroline Clifton-Mogg
2023
Design and photography copyright
© Ryland Peters & Small 2023

Text and photographs in this book have
been previously published by Ryland Peters
& Small in *French Country Living* (2004,
2008) and *Provençal Escapes* (2005, 2009).

See page 190 for full photography credits.

10 9 8 7 6 5 4 3 2 1

ISBN 978-1-78879-520-3

The author's moral rights have been
asserted. All rights reserved.

No part of this publication may be
reproduced, stored in a retrieval system
or transmitted in any form or by any means,
electronic, mechanical, photocopying or
otherwise, without the prior permission of
the publisher.

A CIP record for this book is available
from the British Library.

Library of Congress CIP data has been
applied for.

Printed and bound in China

MIX
Paper | Supporting
responsible forestry
FSC
www.fsc.org   FSC® C008047

1788795202 ✓

CONTENTS

INTRODUCTION

Everyone has their own idea of summer in France. For some, it's the warm, all-pervasive scent of rosemary, thyme, basil and resinous pine trees. For others, it's taste – that fresh, fresh baguette with the irresistible pointed end, known as the *quignon*, torn off and eaten on the way out of the boulangerie; or the sharp olives, the huge scented tomatoes, the flaky croissants. And for others still, it is the small sights – the old fountains in village squares, the weekly street markets, the olive trees and Turkey oaks.

Personally, when I close my eyes and picture summer in France, I'm in the South. The time is about 6 o'clock in the evening and I'm sitting at a small round table in a wicker chair outside one of the cafés underneath the old plane trees that line the street. There's a slightly frosty glass of rosé on the table, and I'm just sitting around and watching: villagers, dogs (so many dogs), children, holidaymakers. I'm very content.

When you drive – or go by train – from northern France to the South, you realize what a large and extraordinarily diverse country you are travelling through. Two-and-a-half times bigger than the island of Great Britain (though still smaller than Texas), France has it all, geographically speaking. Oceans and seas, mountains and forests, rivers and lakes, sand and snow. Somewhere beyond Lyon, the light changes; it becomes luminous, softer and warmer, and the cicadas start to strum. France also has it all both architecturally and decoratively, though you may still encounter a few eccentricities, such as funny hotels in which the fitted carpet extends up the wall to the dado/chair rail.

Over the years, I have spent many happy holidays driving through France armed with a clutch of the amazingly detailed and authoritative Michelin Green Guides. Between them, these little volumes cover every part of the country, pinpointing everything from the sites of battles and sieges to particularly pleasing views as well as fragments of 15th-century wooden altarpieces and Roman basilicas. There is something for everyone within their pages, no matter where your interests lie.

Of course, many people's interests lie with food. It is true that the cuisine in French resturants is perhaps not as universally good as it once was – which, of course, may be because other countries have raised the bar – but the dishes and ingredients that you can buy from markets and in town and village shops are still far better than their equivalents elsewhere. The *traiteurs* with their *plats composés*, their pâtés and hams, their salads and sausages; the patisseries with their fruit tarts, cakes and gateaux; and the market stalls selling everything from fruit and vegetables to roast chicken, langoustines and fresh pasta. These really are some of the glories of France.

It is no wonder, therefore, that so many people want to spend all their summers in France and dream of buying somewhere that they can make their own. The houses featured in this book come in a variety of shapes, sizes and ages; they are large and small, some surrounded by their own land, others closely surrounded by their neighbours in old villages. Some are simply furnished and others really rather luxurious. But they have all been designed with the same aim in mind: to be lived in and enjoyed in the soft, seductive air of La Belle France.

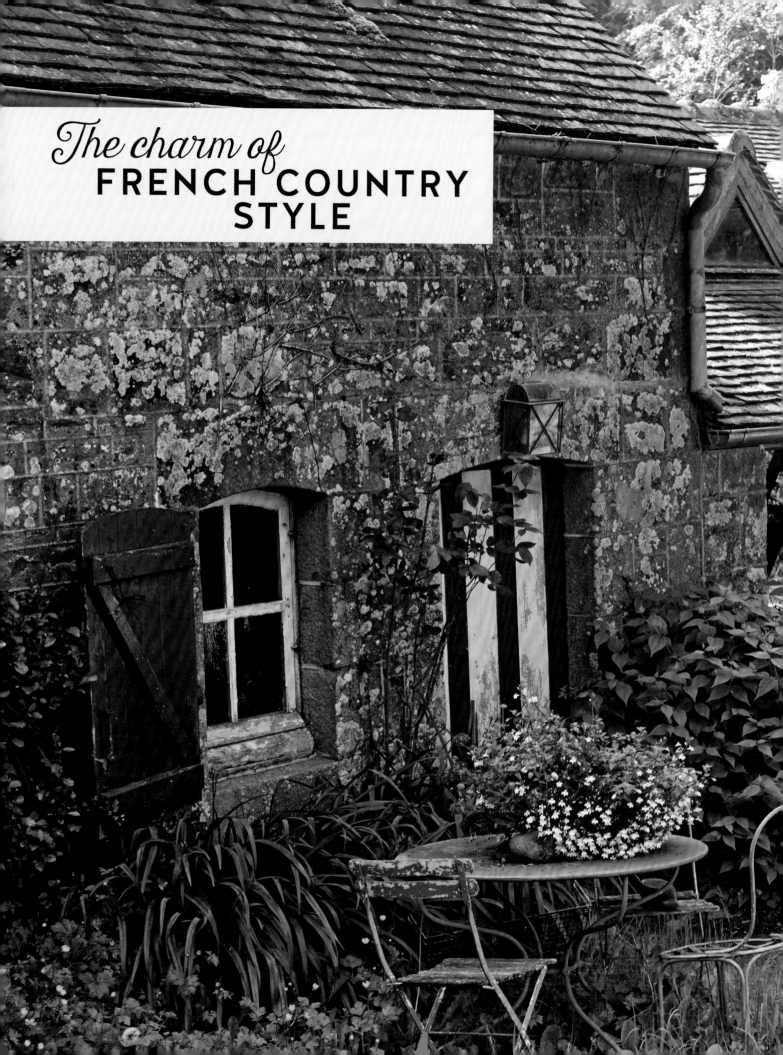

The charm of
FRENCH COUNTRY STYLE

COLOUR

The French rural colour palette is like no other. Soft and almost translucent in appearance, it gives the impression that the base colour has been washed over, creating the effect of a multilayered film of colour over a creamy background.

On first telling, the names of the colours associated with the French country interior sound much like those of colours used anywhere else: blue, grey, cream, green, pink. Simple enough, you might think, but – as always with the French – the difference lies in the way they tell it.

French colours are mixed to a particular subtlety and depth – if that sounds as if they might be boring or dull, nothing could be further from reality. However, it is true that nothing shouts, and there is nothing about the colours that is either flashy or exhibitionist. These are colours that both soothe and evoke interest, that have character and depth, that are designed to alter in different lights – but also always complement and enhance the other elements of a room.

The natural light of a particular terrain affects the way in which decorative colours are perceived. France is a large country, and the light changes dramatically from the north to the south (as well as from east to west). These natural differences are reflected in the way that colours are used – both inside and out. The further north you travel, the more you find shades that are paler and more limpid, echoing the huge northern skies. In the predominantly sunny south, however, the tones are stronger and more definite – reflecting the sharp contrasts to be seen in the surrounding landscape.

Traditionally, of course, the colours used were dependent on the local pigments. Different areas used local ingredients to make the pigments; other traditional recipes included limewashes and milk washes, and grey- or green-toned distemper.

In a high-ceilinged dining room, the first impression is one of colour and contrast. But in fact, there is practically no colour at all: everything from walls to woodwork to furniture and linen is in graduated tones of grey, blue-grey and soft white (*opposite*).

The calm atmosphere in this bedroom is created by the painted wooden walls – finished to look almost powdered. A screen, used as a freestanding headboard, has been covered in a neutral material, and the polished-concrete floor reflects all the colours back (*left*). An exercise in French contemporary classicism: while the colours come from a typical country palette, emphasizing soft blue-greys and whites, there are unusual modern touches such as the painted clock on the wall and the concrete floor (*below*). One of the tricks of success when decorating with a French country palette is to avoid combining sharply contrasting colours. Attempting to create a harmony of complementary tones may be more challenging, but the end result will make it all worthwhile (*opposite*).

White – as a decorative colour rather than a no-choice neutral – has always been favoured by the French. Their oil-based white does not have the cold brilliance of a modern acrylic white, but is instead subtle and sophisticated. It is represented in the white paintwork set off with gilding, as admired by Madame de Pompadour, and the soft whites favoured by Marie-Antoinette when she played at country life in the Petit Hameau; such rustic, gentle tones were supposed to reflect the natural, simple quality of the queen's life away from court (although her idea of simplicity would possibly not have been shared by most of her subjects).

These French whites are sometimes creamy, sometimes touched with grey and often have the soft texture of chalk. Very often several different shades of white were and are used together – a look much admired by the late English decorator John Fowler, for example, who was himself much influenced by the French colour palette of the past. Fowler would combine many different – but only slightly different – tones of white on woodwork and plaster details and in panels; he was always looking for a harmonious, restful, architectural composition that suggested rather than dictated.

The colours in this comfortable living room are neither bold nor intimidating. The cupboard is a fine antique *buffet à deux corps* (one cupboard above another), coloured in soft pinks and greys. The two antique armchairs – known as *chaises à la reine*, and dating from the reign of Louis XV – are left polished and pale (*opposite*). This room was originally the kitchen, hence the pleasing panel of ceramic tiles set into the wall beneath the window. The design echoes in miniature the larger design of tiles on the floor, and every element is kept deliberately low-key (*left*). In this bedroom, the texture of the walls becomes both the colour and the pattern. Applied as a combination of mud and hay, the walls represent a relatively modern version of traditional techniques such as the American 'adobe' finish, and it would be a shame to sully the finish by painting or decorating them further. The unusual floor tiles – made in a traditional design of terracotta bordered with oak fillets – have been reversed to show the original terracotta finish (*below*).

AS YOU TRAVEL NORTH, YOU FIND PALER, MORE LIMPID SHADES
THAT ECHO THE HUGE NORTHERN SKIES; IN THE MOSTLY
SUNNY SOUTH, THE STRONGER, MORE DEFINITE TONES OF PAINT
REFLECT THE SHARP CONTRASTS IN THE LANDSCAPE.

Other neutrals are also popular in the French country palette, but again they always have a subtle twist. Rather than a clear cream, for example, a soft putty colour – cream mixed with an infinitesimal amount of grey – can often be seen. Indeed, grey, whether combined with white or not, is pretty ubiquitous; a pale version of grey was the popular colour of the 17th and early 18th centuries, often contrasted with off-white – an immensely sophisticated combination. This domestic grey is nothing like the institutionalized, rather dead tone so often seen in French municipal buildings, but a more delicate colour – almost luminous, lighter, reflective and often with a pale pink or blue base that gives it a fresh or warm tone. And the colour is often mixed or contrasted with other shades of grey – a chalk grey might be combined with a deeper, dove-wing grey in panels and woodwork, for example, and lifted by touches of creamy white.

From grey comes blue and – except in those interiors influenced by the heat of the Mediterranean – most French blues are reflective, reflecting colours, used to calm and soothe. When grey-blue is not required, an alternative commonly seen is a watery, pale turquoise, again often used in combination with a creamy white.

As with blue, so with green. In nearly all French greens, whether pale or strong, there is a little grey – or sometimes black – in the mixture. Not for France the cheerful emeralds or mown-grass greens of other places. Subtlety is both the goal and the prize.

From grey also come mauve and lilac – either as bright as the viola or iris or closer to the quiet, almost musty tones that are quintessentially French, and which look so winning when teamed with a grey-green, perhaps used on woodwork. A more sophisticated combination that is sometimes seen is a grey-mauve offset by a dark, almost terracotta red – the red known as *sang-de-boeuf* makes a particularly effective contrast.

Pinks and peaches are also to be found among the range of French country colours, but they are not childlike nursery colours – there is nothing of a sugary or sweet nature about them. Like so many French country colours, the pinks and peaches appear almost organic, seeming as though they might have emerged from the colour of the original plaster rather than having been applied on top of it, and again, they often seem to include a hint of pale-grey ancestry.

No country colour palette could be complete without yellow, but French yellows stand apart from their competitors in tone and warmth. The yellows that French people prefer to use in their interiors are on the whole neither too sharp or strident nor too deep; they are the yellows that are easy to live with and acceptable to all – diluted chrome yellow, saffron mixed with white and butter yellow softened, appropriately, with cream.

In this corridor leading into the brick-floored room where winter logs are stored, all the wooden surfaces have been painted slightly different shades of blue to give a subtle effect (*opposite above*). A symphony in sage, with grey-green used in different strengths: slightly deeper on the woodwork and chimneypiece, as well as on the painted floor.

Slightly paler on the painted beams – a harmonious whole (*opposite below*). This room takes its cue from the worn pink of the terracotta floor tiles and from the plastered wall and painted panelling. In the same palette, the daybed has stripes of clover and rose with abundant cushions in Indienne and toile de Jouy designs (*above*).

Then there are the decorative colour combinations – those important marriages of woodwork and wall. It is rare in France – at any rate, among exponents of this particular style – to observe a strong, violent or dramatic contrast in a room. A subtle combination, something that pleases or interests and which incorporates other elements of the room is preferred. The French have never felt that the only colour for woodwork is white – in fact, in many cases, they consciously shy away from this most obvious of tones. If white is used, it will be an off-white, but it is just as likely to be grey, or it may be green or blue, or sometimes a mixture of the two.

In a French country house, all the interior elements that are made of wood – not just the architectural surrounds – may be coated in paint. Like the Scandinavians, the French particularly like painted furniture, and the soft and subtle colours they favour are as effective on furniture as they are on walls; to the French, a painted finish is as charming, if not more so, than the patina of old wood. Dedicated paint strippers take note: in the 17th, 18th and 19th centuries, furniture was, as often as not, painted – and those who today religiously strip back any painted pine piece they find in the name of authenticity are often destroying its charm by changing it into something that it was never intended to be.

Yellow ochre is a true earth colour found naturally in rocks and soil that has been used on walls (and in caves) for thousands of years. Because of its closeness to nature, it is the most amenable of shades, bringing warmth to every surface. Here it is used in a bedroom and adjoining bathroom, and anchored with warm terracotta tiles (*opposite*). It also makes an effective background for pieces of local green-glazed pottery, and is applied to raw plaster walls above stone steps and a painted skirting board/baseboard (*this page*).

MATERIALS

The materials typical of French country style seem to come from the landscape itself, from the surrounding countryside, where natural life predominates. Wood, stone, terracotta and metals – these are materials as old as the land itself and have been continuously used since dwellings were first constructed there.

Nowhere in true French country style can the link between the past and the present be more clearly seen than in the choice of materials utilized both inside and outside the home.

The emphasis on natural materials means that the combination of textures chosen is very important. When everything stems from the same natural core, harmony is attainable – indeed, pretty difficult not to attain. Floors are basically bare, which allows the material of the floor – whether it be stone, terracotta or wood – to provide the interest; floor rugs range from the simplest of plaited/braided or woven grasses to decorative antique rugs whose old beauty is flattered by the simplicity of the floor.

A wide variety of woods is evident in rural interiors, but the woods used in different parts of France were and are largely those from the trees growing in the surrounding countryside: fruitwoods such as walnut and cherry, alongside traditional

hardwoods such as oak and elm. Exotics such as mahogany or maple will not be found in abundance here, for self-sufficiency is the name of the game.

In true French country style, wood is ubiquitous and the most popular material, used both indoors and out. Outside, as well as the obvious doors and windows, in almost every region of the country, exterior wooden shutters are used, not just for their practical qualities but also, and this is characteristically French, as what can only be called a design statement – carefully painted in a colour that is often unexpectedly strong and that contrasts boldly with the more traditional façade.

A terracotta floor, particularly one of a certain age, brings instant warmth into a room – no rugs required! The unevenness of the tiles, the variations in tone and the reflection of daylight onto the floor are all immensely satisfying to look at (*opposite*).

Wide oak floorboards that have been stained reflect the colour of the ceiling beams. The translucent white hangings of the iron bedstead are a suitable foil for the rather heavy floor (*opposite*). Painted panelling, by its very nature, brings a warm element to a space. Used here in a room that may not have started life as a bathroom, it brings a touch of comfort to a scheme that otherwise consists mainly of hard surfaces (*right*).

Inside, skirtings/baseboards and surrounds are wooden, and wooden-framed furniture – indelibly associated with French taste – is seen everywhere. Much built-in furniture is also made of wood, again sometimes stained or polished, but usually coloured in a sympathetic tone. Sturdy wooden beams – more often than not exposed – are sometimes left in their natural state but are more usually painted or colour-stained; it is all part of French country style.

No discussion of French interiors could pass without mention of wood panelling; whether painted or polished, it is one of the greatest decorating devices known. It can correct faults of scale in a room, add gravitas where none existed and give emphasis in the subtlest of ways. Why do we always associate wood panelling with French interior decoration? After all, other countries use panels, wood

or plaster, in their decorative schemes, but there is something fundamentally French about the idea of panelling, even when it is actually trompe l'oeil.

Wooden floors are laid in houses throughout France, both in the country and in the town, and since French country style eschews fitted carpets, the finish of any wooden floor is highly significant. It might be wood-stained, sealed and polished, waxed, limed or coloured – either with a painted finish or a tinted stain. The look is natural, the colour rarely strong, for the important element is that the wood discreetly draws attention.

Very often in France, indeed as often as possible, local stone is used as a floor paving inside the house. The thought of this may bring a shiver to many of us who live under northern skies, but stone is not, in fact, as cold as it is painted (or should that be polished?).

The joy and beauty of stone lies in being able to appreciate its variations and range of tones, which come about when it has been cut or chiselled in a sympathetic manner. Although new stone takes time to weather well, old stone – and it does not have to be very old – has a softness and variety that is immensely appealing.

Hand-cut stone is obviously preferable to the machine-made version, and indeed there are few examples of the latter to be seen in the French countryside. When paving stones are old, subdued, warm and glimmering, there is little to trump them.

UNPLASTERED STONE WALLS, PERHAPS
NOT SEEN AS FREQUENTLY TODAY AS
THEY ONCE WERE, MAY SOMETIMES – IF
PROPERLY TREATED – SEEM TO SHIMMER
WITH A SHADOWY SOFTNESS THAT
CAN BE MOST APPEALING.

When left uncovered, stone tends to dominate a room and requires
sturdy furniture to balance it. Here, a large traditional bookcase brings
scale and proportion to the setting (*opposite*). Natural materials make
their own colour scheme, particularly when sympathetically combined
with other elements. In this bedroom, untreated stone walls in tones of
light grey give impact to a dark grey painted wooden chest. The success
of the scheme depends on the contrast of tone and texture, as well as
cleverly placed pictures and lamps (*right*). This stone wall has been
cleverly handled by having an iron-framed seat placed in front of it and
piled with cushions in the same tones as the wall. This is far subtler than
trying to use contrasting colours (*below*).

BOTH TERRACOTTA AND BRICK HAVE A SENSUOUS WARMTH
THAT DERIVES FROM THEIR COLOURS AND FROM THEIR TACTILE
PRESENCE. THE ROMANS ARE, AS ALWAYS, CREDITED WITH
HAVING BEEN THE FIRST TO USE THESE MATERIALS.

A cobbled stone floor, although sometimes difficult to walk on, brings a wonderful textural quality to the formal appearance of this living room and highlights the close-beamed ceiling (*above*). Nothing is more welcoming than a floor of handmade bricks in varying tones and shapes. The bricks lead on to square and then hexagonal terracotta tiles. An earthy feast! (*opposite*).

Although most stone lovers are happy with carefully cut rectangular slabs, for aficionados of decorative stone, the most satisfactory use of the material is on the floor in the form of cobbles – inside rather than outside the home – where the rounded shape of each stone brings texture as well as a sculptural quality to a room.

Since clay is found throughout France, terracotta – particularly in the form of tiles – is ubiquitous. Although strictly speaking a man-made rather than an entirely natural material, terracotta has acquired credibility from its long history – it has been made for thousands of years, and used both inside and outside. The Romans are, as always, credited with being the first to have produced it.

Terracotta and its close companion brick are characterized by a sensuous warmth that comes from both the colour and the tactile presence of the materials; even terracotta tiles that have been finished with a modern sealant have a friendly, comforting feeling – a sense of elemental earth, which is, after all, what the material intrinsically is.

Terracotta floor tiles come in several traditional shapes – not only large and small squares but also long, thin, paver-style rectangles and hexagonal shapes. They can be glazed, and smaller-version glazed terracotta tiles are often used for wall and surface tiles as well as for covering floors. The glazes often appear artlessly simple – just a hint of the original clay appearing beneath a patchy washed surface – but, like so much in the French country style, the subtle final effect is carefully thought out and achieved only with skill and taste.

Would it be an exaggeration to say that a house that has been designed or evolved in the French country style could hardly be in the running were there not some metal incorporated somewhere in the scheme? A little strong, perhaps, but there has long been in France an affinity with metal that is not necessarily shared by other nations. Traditionally, it was the *ferronier* whose art and skill wrought and cast the iron into sympathetic and beautiful shapes – and the material is just as popular today in and around the house as it was 300 years ago.

Quite apart from its use in making occasional furniture – think of those little round outdoor tables and twisted chairs so beloved of cartoonists – metal is used in the windows and on the stairs. There are bowed and bulbous window grilles and sinuous stair rails and banisters, as well as kitchen fittings and door furniture. Somehow the craftsmen seem to be able to forge and turn the material into designs that, although complex, are also light and airy, sometimes with an almost rococo feel.

A relatively new material that is now widely seen in the French country interior is concrete, sometimes plastered or polished, sometimes left in its pristine glory. Used to make built-in furniture – perhaps a seat or a storage unit or in the kitchen a sturdy sink unit – concrete can be coloured and textured to work with the rest of the room.

Around the metal outdoor table is a set of French bistro chairs. Widely used, particularly in the warm South, these chairs were first designed in the late 19th century and can be found with either wooden or metal slatted seats (*opposite*). A typically French stone and wooden semi-spiral staircase of the 1800s, its sweeping curves held by cast-iron railings. The stairs contrast with the traditional stone tiles on the hall floor (*above*). Metal has always been used in French country kitchens, from jugs/pitchers in pewter or tin to hard-wearing metal plates and chargers (*right and far right*).

FURNITURE

French country furniture is extremely well adapted to its function, and each piece is polished or painted to show off its lines to best effect. Traditional, natural materials are always used, and the pieces themselves seem strangely organic – as if they are growing up from the earth in rounded, comfortable shapes.

The characteristic pieces of furniture found in a French country house, whether the dwelling is large or small, combine immense charm with intense practicality. Traditionally, it was the obvious practical solution to use local woods to make local furniture, and that remains the case. In northern and central France, light-toned fruitwoods such as cherry and walnut are found, as well as occasionally (and more often in the south) olive or mulberry wood.

But although French country furniture is based on the natural materials to hand, and is designed to play its part in the country house, it would be wrong to describe it as rustic – a word that can often imply a twee, almost painful self-consciousness. A better word would be rural, which could be defined as simple in style and designed for a specific purpose. Think of the benches, tables, straight-backed dressers/hutches and armoires that

can be found in almost every French country home; they look as though they belong and are happy to be in place. That is, in fact, the case, since the story of furniture design throughout history is the story of adaptation: pieces originally commissioned for the rich and fashionable were, over time, adapted and simplified for use in less exalted households. From seating to storage, from the buffet to the armoire, designs and styles emerged that have stood the test of time and are still made today. But they are not clumsy: there is in country pieces as well as in city pieces a delicacy about French furniture that is often lacking in the English equivalent.

An ornamental commode dating from the 18th century has been both decorated and painted in a fairly intricate fashion. Its decorative appearance means that it is most effectively displayed as here – on a floor of stone slabs and simply flanked by a pair of branched sconces (*opposite*).

ALTHOUGH THEY ARE NOTHING IF NOT PRACTICAL AND
SUPREMELY WELL ADAPTED TO THEIR PARTICULAR FUNCTION,
PIECES OF FRENCH COUNTRY FURNITURE ARE ALSO IMMENSELY
DECORATIVE AND EASY TO LIVE WITH.

The imposing all-purpose armoire in this bedroom has been put to use as a clothes cupboard. The size of the piece – painted, in the traditional manner – means that the room requires little additional furniture other than a wooden table and rush-seated chair (*opposite*). In this living room, a colour palette characteristic of French country style has been used, with soft blues, greys and whites on walls and furniture. The only hint of pattern to be seen in the room is in the subtle colour and designs of the rugs that have been laid on the polished wooden floor (*right*).

There is a certain subtlety of line that is unique, and which has something to do with the materials used as well as the lightness of touch within the design.

The style has become famous; there are one or two almost iconic designs that can be found throughout rural (and not so rural) France that are just as sought after today as they ever were. Take perhaps the most instantly recognizable piece in any French household, the armoire – the large wooden storage cupboard that could, and can, be used in any room. Upstairs, an armoire is usually used for the storage of linen and clothing, and in the kitchen for storing kitchenware or food – although when used as a *garde-manger*, or larder, it often appears in the form of a lower cupboard with doors surmounted with open shelves, perhaps protected by a chicken-wire grill.

This useful object – a cupboard combined with open shelves – can be found today in any room in the French country house: in the living room holding books and objects, in the kitchen as a holder of dishes and cooking equipment, in the bedroom with linen and other essentials and in halls and on landings as general repositories of belongings.

Such cupboards are sometimes limewashed, painted or colour-stained. The inside surfaces might be painted, or lined with patterned paper or fabric. There is also a small *garde-manger* that looks like a wooden, wire-fronted cage and was customarily hung from the ceiling or high on the wall to keep the contents out of sight of hungry people.

The buffet, or low cupboard, is another popular piece of furniture that was traditionally used for both storage and display. Frequently designed with serpentine curves, the buffet sometimes has an upper tier that might be simply shelves, or might be another, smaller cupboard, when it is known as a *buffet à deux corps*. Like the armoire, it can be of polished or painted wood, and otherwise decorated or adorned with carving or paintings.

Until the 17th century, in most countries, chairs were still straight-backed, formal objects, designed to reflect the status of the sitter and to command respect rather than to offer comfort. But in France, something was afoot.

A new type of seat was in the process of being invented – something that made sitting a pleasure rather than a necessity; indeed, it would not be inaccurate to say that the French invented the armchair.

From France came the comfortable, low-backed, feather-stuffed armchair; the *bergère*, a tub chair with upholstered arms and cushions; the *marquise*, a loveseat; the *canapé*, an intimate sofa; and the chaise longue, on which hours could be spent enjoying the latest fashionable novels – all designed for relaxation and enjoyment.

Although now overtaken by the ubiquitous upholstered sofa, the rush-seated banquette is still sometimes seen today, and much sought after in its antique incarnation. Known in France as a *radassié*, this type of banquette looks like an extended wooden-backed armchair and convivially seats three or four.

On a simple painted Louis XV cupboard and against an antique wooden panel is an 18th-century painting. On either side of the cupboard stand two antique faux marble columns (*above*). This is a living room in all senses, encompassing as it does both an area for sitting and relaxing and a table at which to eat. The traditional sofa is made even more comfortable with the addition of subtly coloured cushions and matching throw (*right*). In an old house in the Luberon, the living room opens onto a small courtyard. A bench in the Provençal style sits across from a chair designed by the 19th-century furniture maker Michael Thonet (*opposite*).

DURING THE 17TH CENTURY, THE FRENCH INVENTED THE
ARMCHAIR, AN INVITING SEAT THAT TRANSFORMED SITTING
FROM A NECESSITY INTO A PLEASURE.

A colour immediately associated with French country style is warm rose madder, one of the dyes used in the printing of traditional toiles. Made into a generous bedcover, the toile is picked up by the checked rug on the floor (*opposite*). An old basin has had a curtain gathered around it, making a space for storage. The whole area is decorated more as a corner of a bedroom than as a bathroom (*right*).

The French country style bed is many things, but what it is not is a divan/box spring with an upholstered base that extends to the floor. It may be made from metal or wood, but it will be freestanding, and it will almost always have both a head and a foot, perhaps finished in a distinctive decorative style. This has always been the case. Traditionally, beds were symbolic as well as utilitarian pieces – often highly decorated and ornamented. Although not loaded with quite so much symbolism today, the bed still represents one of the largest and most important pieces of furniture in the house, and therefore is often decorated and – if it has posts – draped accordingly.

A lesser piece, but one that is instantly recognizable as belonging to the French country style, is the marble-topped washstand to be found not only in bathrooms and kitchens but also in halls or on landings – anywhere where a basin or sink may be installed. These are nothing if not sleek updates from the past; where once the basin would have been a portable bowl in a set with a jug/pitcher, now it is an inset polished bowl, complete with taps/faucets.

The photographs in this book make it clear that there are very few pieces that look as if they have just landed haphazardly in a room. Whether it is a formal reception room, a bedroom or even a kitchen or bathroom, the furniture in a French country house has to be chosen – each item with care – because each piece matters very much. Yet what doesn't matter is whether it is new or old or a combination of both – it is the look and the purpose that counts.

There has never been a barrier between old and new in French country style. Perhaps that is because, although the furniture may be rural in concept, there is an undoubted sophistication to it – an innate delicacy and subtlety of line that is unique to the French, and which manifests itself in the materials used as well as in the lightness of touch applied to colour and finish. French country furniture is immediately recognizable; although it is nothing if not practical and supremely adapted to its particular function, it is also immensely decorative and easy to live with.

FABRICS

Traditional textile designs and patterns are far from scorned by lovers of French country style: they are still produced today. They may sometimes be recoloured or brightened, but the designs that were first made widely available during the 18th and 19th centuries are just as popular as they ever were.

French rural interiors are dominated, albeit subtly, by fabrics. Textile designs and colours, and the inventive use of fabrics throughout the home, are a vital part of the entire look. In every room, textiles appear in profusion – not just as curtains and blinds but on chairs, over benches, as cushions and on beds and tables. As expressions of both colour and design, fabrics lift every other element in the room.

It is fascinating that designs for textiles created in the 18th and 19th centuries are appreciated just as much in modern times – both in the city and the countryside – as when they were first taken from the blocks. It is a testament to the brilliance of these early designs that today – whether recoloured or newly reproduced in the original colourways – they can still blend in with and often enhance modern design and decorative schemes.

Designs range from small, precise, geometrically governed patterns to stripes of every size and colour. There are romantic florals – sometimes hugely oversized and reminiscent of an overgrown garden – and vast scenic prints such as the familiar designs associated with the toiles de Jouy.

Toiles de Jouy are as irrevocably associated with French interiors as croissants are with French breakfasts. Even among those people who do not immediately recognize the name of Jouy, there can be no mistaking the designs.

Even the smallest piece of antique textile can inspire decorative ideas if you use lateral thinking. In this bedroom, an old scalloped pelmet/valance, presumably once one of a pair, has been used to beautify very simple, very long curtains. Although the fabric gives the room a lift, it is not strong enough to overwhelm the simple scheme (*opposite*).

TEXTILES ARE SEEN IN PROFUSION – AS CURTAINS, BLINDS AND CUSHIONS, ON CHAIRS, OVER BENCHES, ON BEDS AND TABLES. AS EXPRESSIONS OF COLOUR AND DESIGN, THEY LIFT EVERY OTHER ELEMENT IN THE ROOM.

This bedroom under the eaves, with its sloping ceiling and exposed beams, has a bed with a carved wooden headboard painted in traditional grey, and a quilted, flowered *boutis*. The curtains are tied back with toile de Jouy in the same soft tones of pink (*opposite*). Simplicity always triumphs over complexity in the French country style. The simple design of these curtains works well with the flower-printed wallpaper; hooked simply onto rings, they need no lining, since external shutters diffuse the light (*left*). Three different designs have been incorporated in this small area – an approach that, decoratively speaking, is rarely recommended. Yet because they have been carefully chosen – and even though the cushions are in a toile design and the window seat and chair are in coordinating stripes and checks – the final effect is pleasing to the eye (*below*).

In the middle of the 18th century, Christophe-Philippe Oberkampf started a manufactory using copper plates to print cottons at Jouy-en-Josas, a village on the road between Paris and Versailles. The popular taste for printed designs on cotton had already been determined with the importation a century earlier, through the French East India Company, of calicos and chintzes – known as Indiennes, after their land of origin. So popular were these new textiles throughout France that they were seen as a threat to the Lyons silk-weaving industry, and a ban – which was in place for 50 years – was imposed on the manufacture or sale of all printed cottons both imported and produced at home.

As soon as the ban was lifted, Oberkampf was one of the first to take advantage of the new freedom, and in 1760 opened his works, later employing Jean-Baptiste Huet, one of the great designers of his time, to create exciting new designs for the receptive public. The factory was soon enjoying huge success; the new copper plates for printing were far larger than earlier models, which meant that the designs could be wider in scale, up to a square metre (around 11 square feet) in area.

Country textiles all share an affinity of design and of colour; stored in a fat pile when not in use, these quilted covers and traditional eiderdowns look as pretty as they are comfortable (*far left*). Indigo – the steely blue-grey used on toiles de Jouy – is here employed as part of a bedcover with matching cushion (*left*). Variations on a theme: an antique daybed has been dressed in a a fragile, soft blue print on the seat and, for the cushions, a stronger, reworked ticking design in deep blue and white. The diamond-shaped floor tiles become part of the overall design (*below left*).

Huet capitalized on this by creating designs that ranged from chinoiserie fantasies to antique follies, pastoral scenes and even military triumphs. Napoleon was a great admirer of Jouy designs, and several of his military campaigns were immortalized as printed cottons – as well as other popular events and games and sports of the day.

In one sense, those famous toiles sum up French textiles: appearing at first sight almost artlessly simple, with their limited palette and monochromatic combinations, with designs that are recognizable metres away, these toiles are actually deeply sophisticated. In the best examples, the colorations are incredibly subtle. The blue is not just any blue – it is an inky, grey-touched blue; the red is madder with other tones in it; the violet is tinted with other shades; and the brown is as soft as 19th-century drawing ink.

The Indiennes that were produced by the enterprising Oberkampf in the 18th century, which feature motifs based on traditional Indian and Eastern textiles – including the adaptable and ever-popular 'Tree of Life' design – also remain very popular today, with many designs combining geometric and floral motifs. In addition, it is still possible to find literally hundreds of variations of small regular flower designs – the sort of pattern that is often associated just with the South of France but which actually occurs throughout the country, and that comes from a peasant tradition of design.

'*Faites simple*', usually attributed to the 19th-century chef Auguste Escoffier, is just as applicable to interiors as it is to food. This bedroom is perfectly simple and perfectly comfortable. From the beamed ceiling the bed has been hung with linen curtains, actually antique sheets. They are slotted onto metal rods attached to the ceiling by a central trapeze. Comfortable chairs on a terracotta tiled floor complete the picture (*right*).

Although stripes are international and timeless, there are two stripes that seem more representative of France than any others. The first is traditional mattress ticking; this was originally confined to blue and grey, but is now available in several modern variations. The second is not actually one stripe; rather, it is a design incorporating several stripes of different widths, and frequently comes in subtle colour combinations of blue, buff, old pink and cream. Both variations are much used to cover fitted or squab seat cushions throughout the house, as well as in blinds and simple curtains.

What is important is that, whether old or new, all these textiles are, in French country style, always used with restraint. At the window, elaborately made and designed curtains with swags and tails are rarely seen; more usual are unadorned curtains hung from metal poles, although they are often embellished with quirky brackets and finials. Sometimes a scalloped or straight-edged pelmet/valance is hung across the top of a window frame – particularly effective when it is a piece of antique toile de Jouy.

Boutis are enthusiastically used both on beds (for which they were originally designed), as throws and covers on sofas and chairs and as dress cloths for tables. *Boutis* were traditionally bedspreads or quilts – made, as their British and American counterparts were, as warm decorative coverings for beds, and often embellished with accomplished and elaborate stitching. The antique version of *boutis* are avidly collected today, but new ones, in the same soft colour combinations, can also be found and work very well, especially when several are used in combination.

Antique textiles themselves are much collected in France. Brocante fairs – a cross between junk and antique sales – are held throughout France on a daily basis, and there are many antique shops that specialize in textiles of all types. Many of these are based in L'Isle-sur-la-Sorgue, a town in Provence that is a country antique lovers' paradise.

Antique textiles generally are much in evidence in French country interiors. For many devotees, no piece is too small or too insignificant to be used somewhere. Not only is toile de Jouy collected, but other, lesser-known toiles such as toile de Beautiran and toile de Rouen are also sought after. All of these textiles are made up into cushions, of course – both floppy ones and neat, tailored squab cushions used on rush- or cane-seated chairs – and pieces that are too small even for a cushion might feature as central panels in a larger piece. Textile pieces are used draped over beds, sometimes over a *boutis*, as well as to cover headboards, and they are also seen as runners on buffets and chests.

Old linen sheets – which even today are relatively easy to find, although becoming rarer – are much prized, too, particularly those that are monogrammed and embroidered. They still serve as sheets but also as bed covers. They may also be used as tablecloths or as starched, unlined, lightweight curtains; even when a sheet is damaged, a decorative use can nevertheless be found for it – it may be cut up and used as cushion covers.

TOILES DE JOUY ARE AS IRREVOCABLY ASSOCIATED WITH FRENCH INTERIORS AS CROISSANTS ARE WITH FRENCH BREAKFASTS. EVEN AMONG PEOPLE UNFAMILIAR WITH THE NAME, THERE CAN BE NO MISTAKING THE DESIGNS.

By being stretched, hung and displayed across an old wooden door, an antique wall hanging introduces a surprising and innovative decorative touch to what would otherwise have been a plain corner (*above*). A collection of old textiles – here stored in the ubiquitous armoire – can be made to look attractive even when not in use or on display. In this instance, the different designs have been stacked according to colour and pattern, creating an interesting and decorative design (*right*). Another reason for the compatibility between different patterns and designs is that strong colour contrasts are rare. On this Louis XV daybed there are two quilts – one antique, the other new – as well as cushions in different fabrics, including some made in an 18th-century toile de Beautiran (*opposite*).

DECORATIVE DETAILS

Every object used to decorate and adorn French country interiors was first made with another function in mind – another life, in fact. Few things of beauty are discarded in the French country home; when an item loses its usefulness, it can still be admired as a decorative object, particularly if it has acquired some of the patina that comes from years of use.

Those objects that are loosely known as accessories – the decorative wherewithals that give a house its individuality and character – are alive and well in the French country house, but they are accessories with a difference. In keeping with the ethos behind the style of the French country house, there are few pieces to be seen that have been selected for their decorative value alone – which is not to say that they lack elegance. There is an elegance, of course – why wouldn't there be? – but it is the elegance of use rather than the elegance of ornamentation.

Ceramics, glass and metalware are to be seen everywhere in the French country home. The pieces look neither fragile nor mean of spirit; cups and glasses are easy to grasp, plates stack into satisfying piles. First and foremost, they have definite shapes – shapes to enjoy using as well as looking at.

Rather fittingly, considering French people's preoccupation with cooking and eating, anything and everything connected with the kitchen is used as added decoration – from glass storage jars grouped to make a chunky composition or china jugs/pitchers filled with garden flowers to baskets stacked one inside the other in a heap. In one room there may be a group of assorted jugs/pitchers and drinking glasses; in another, earthenware cooking pots of different sizes and shapes or metalwork baskets filled with eggs or fruit.

Gargoulettes (two-handled water vessels), tureens, *tians*, dairy bowls, jugs/pitchers, platters and chargers; all designed to be practical . But these pieces of Provençal pottery with their glowing green glazes are also immensely attractive and gathered together, as seen here, make a lovely display of form and colour (*opposite*).

Collections of decorated coffee- and teapots are grouped on chest tops, and large and small candlesticks are used on chimney pieces and tables. It is simply a question of imagination – and of looking at familiar objects in a different, more lateral light.

Glass is enthusiastically collected everywhere in the world, but in France it is seen predominantly as an expression of the pleasures of the table, rather than something to be hidden away in closed cabinets. Wine glasses and other glasses are often stored outside the kitchen cupboards, on windowsills or tables, where their

lines and designs can be admired; carafes and decanters, too, are often grouped together in a pleasant composition, ready to be pressed into use.

Glazed earthenware cooking dishes and pots may be handed down from generation to generation and are highly prized. In the French countryside they are not banished to the kitchen but are used throughout the house, with the most decorative examples being displayed with pride on bureaux and buffets.

Jugs/pitchers, the original all-purpose containers, are used in every room, and not simply for holding liquids. Filled with flowers or just grouped on shelves and tables according to colour or shape, they are the answer to instant decorating French country style – all jugs/pitchers and carafes are generous and flowing of line, often quirky in design and automatically convey a strong decorative presence.

Large urns and jars of stoneware or glass – the sort of container traditionally used to store olive oil – are particularly popular in French country decorating. Simple and striking, they are put on the floor, underneath tables or in a corner by a staircase or door, for example, or placed on top of cupboards and bookcases, both to give height to a piece and to add depth to the room. They are also much in demand on the terrace or in the garden.

Against a background of old and new tiles, an antique relief-moulded jug/pitcher is used as a decorative container for knives and spoons (*opposite above*). A striking arrangement has been created using simple urns and jars. They form part of a larger composition involving a pair of candelabra and other decorative objects. More delicate items would have had no impact in this robust setting (*opposite below*). Assorted plates are grouped together with a decorative tile on a hanging shelf above a table (*above*). A decorative tureen, pedestal dish and plates all in antique creamware are kept in a space off the kitchen of an old former farmhouse (*right*). Old cutlery/flatware, admired for its shape, is kept in a worn and well-used kitchen table drawer (*far right*).

A milk-glass shade on an iron stand looks like a well-starched tutu (*far left*). Different coloured glass drops can always be combined into a piece of charm, as in this pretty sconce (*left*). The more a chandelier resembles a beautiful necklace, the more it appeals; this one, with its looped garlands, is perfectly placed in a room decorated with a flowered-column paper and set off with an ancestral portrait (*below left*). An ornate chimney piece and panelled walls are further embellished by a collection of antique curtain pole finials, brackets and tiebacks. They appear like ancient treasure from an archaeological dig (*opposite*).

Although there is much fine porcelain made in France – think of the ornate wonders of Sèvres porcelain – in the country, stoneware and tin-glazed earthenware, known as *faïence*, are more easily obtainable and, to many people, preferable. They also work far better decoratively in a country interior than more delicate pieces. Different regions of France produce their own variations of *faïence*, but generally they can be found with deep-coloured glazes – typically an intense mustard yellow, a dark rich green or a soft creamy white through which the basic clay can be seen.

Hand-painted *faïence*, from centres like Moustiers, and creamware – earthenware with a cream body, first made in the 18th century to imitate porcelain – is also widely collected, and can often be seen in country rooms, piled up or displayed individually.

In a group, even cooking pots and pans are used to make a decorative statement – particularly when they are of well-buffed copper. Bowls, saucepans, colanders and skillets are hung, either on the wall or from the hooks of a ceiling-suspended rack. Other metalware includes the twisted and woven baskets sometimes used for storing eggs – and even, occasionally, old wire whisks, collected together and hung on a board above the kitchen sink; the different shapes and sizes of the twirling whisks make a pleasing and witty composition.

Although pictures can be seen on some of the walls in these homes, they tend not to be hung in quantity nor grouped closely together in a geometric composition.

The enormous mirror has been given a starring role from an unusual perspective. Placed on the floor between two windows, the ornately framed looking glass reflects the bed and the arresting decorative piece – a cross between a wheatsheaf and a sunburst – that hangs above the bed (*opposite*). Decorative features in this imposing bedroom derive from the architecture, with the deep green painted and gilded door and the panel above the fireplace painted a contrasting terracotta shade. The room's only decorative accessory is a line of fat candles (*left*). These elaborate sconces, draped with necklaces of crystal, have been hung, in traditional fashion, on either side of a mirror, where their colour tones have been chosen to echo and complement the gesso-based gilded mirror frame (*below*).

MIRRORS ARE USED WITH FLAMBOYANCE IN EVERY ROOM:
GILDED MIRRORS, OVERSIZED MIRRORS, MIRRORS LIKE SUNS,
MIRRORS LIKE GARLANDS; THEY ARE EVERYWHERE, REFLECTING
LIGHT FROM OUTSIDE BACK INTO THE ROOMS.

That is French city style – in the country, such matters are treated more subtly, with one large picture, or perhaps a pair, hung in close conjunction with a piece of furniture or other objects. It will be seen as part of a group, and there will be a meaning in its position.

Mirrors, on the other hand, are not so subtle. They are used with flamboyance in every room: gilded mirrors, oversized mirrors, mirrors like suns, mirrors like garlands; they are everywhere, reflecting light from outside back into the rooms.

No thoughts about the style of decoration in the French countryside would be complete without mention of the most accessible and attractive accessory of all, plants and flowers. Every room has something green and living somewhere – from a basil plant in a pot in the kitchen to mixed bunches of garden flowers or cut branches of flowering shrubs. In buckets and goblets, jugs/pitchers and tubs, usually artfully unarranged, flowers set the true French country tone, and complete the connection between garden and house.

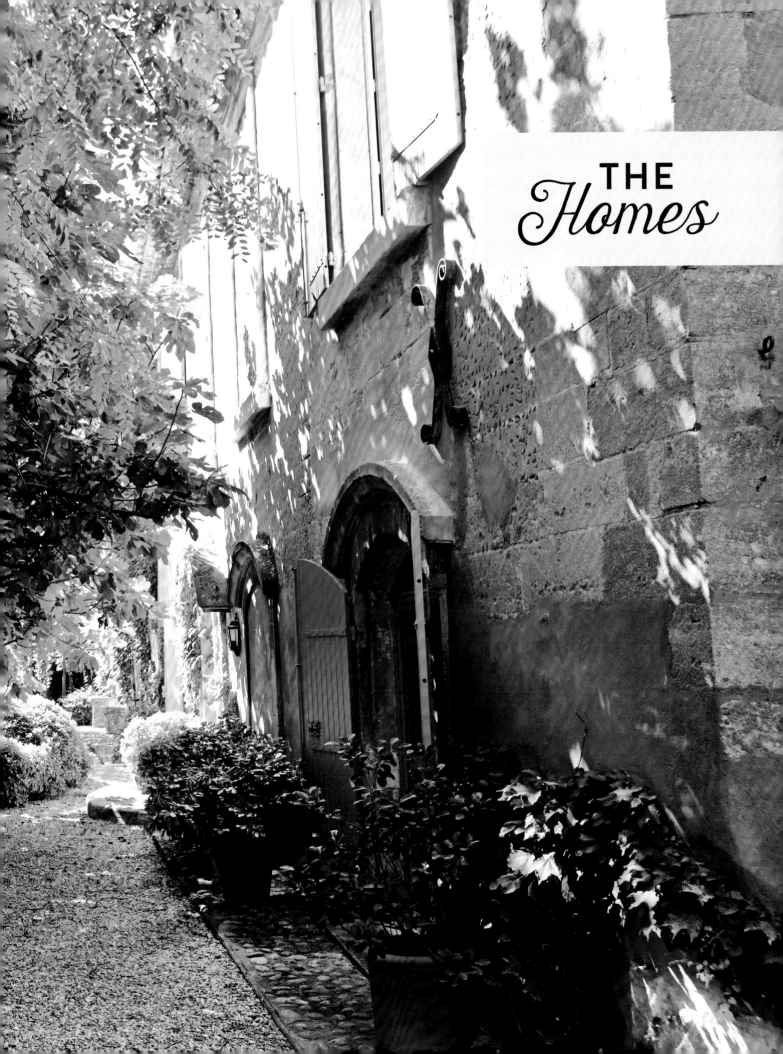

THE
Homes

FAIRY-TALE PAVILION

The American decorator Kenyon Kramer lives outside Aix-en-Provence in a perfect classical pavilion – which isn't actually classical at all. The story of how it came to be is a very French one – almost worthy of a *conte de fées* by the old French teller of fairy tales Charles Perrault.

Kenyon Kramer works in Aix-en-Provence with the renowned French interior and landscape designer Jean-Louis Raynaud. Like most successful designers, Jean-Louis is a man who knows what he likes, and when he spotted near Carpentras – about 60 miles from Aix – a ruined 18th-century hunting lodge, built by a former archbishop of Avignon, he knew that he liked it and wanted it – just not exactly there. So he bought it and transported it stone by old stone to a field near Aix, where he reconstructed it in all its former glory, surrounding it with a fine garden.

All that it lacked was the pair of pavilions that would usually have flanked a lodge of that period. Happily for a designer in search of inspiration, Aix is filled with beautiful buildings from the 17th and 18th centuries, and it was not long before Jean-Louis discovered, either side of the spectacular Pavillon Vendôme, a pair of tiny, exquisite gatehouses, beguiling but in a state of disrepair. Jean-Louis knew they would work perfectly as adjuncts to the hunting lodge. However, this time, instead of uprooting them physically, he decided merely to reproduce the design.

Built as an adjunct to a neighbouring 18th-century hunting lodge, the pavilion has the settled appearance both of old age and no age, with its classical heavy stone lintels and wide glass fanlights (*right*).

The double doors open into an entrance hall covered in a vibrant, madder-toned toile de Jouy called La Toile villageoise, which opens up the space. At the far end is a spiral mahogany staircase; a section of the beamed ceiling can be removed in order to pass furniture between floors (*opposite*). The tiny ground floor of the pavilion is oddly seductive and enticing, and appears larger than it actually is – an effect achieved in part by the ubiquitous use of the toile (in a warm shade; the classic grey-blue would not have worked nearly as well). The other triumph is in the selection of objects, prints and furniture. The dining chairs, once ballroom chairs, are just the right proportions for the 1950s Jansen tole table. The seamless use of toile – not only in curtains, cushions and walls but also on the banquette – extends the boundaries of the room (*right and overleaf*).

'IT IS THE PERFECT HOUSE,' SAYS KENYON KRAMER. 'EVERYONE WHO VISITS WANTS IT; BECAUSE THE SCALE IS SO GOOD, YOU FEEL GOOD, AND KNOW THIS IS HOW YOU WANT TO LIVE.'

He first consulted with La Commission des monuments historiques, the body that cares for historic buildings in France. (After he had finished the project, the Commission restored the originals – giving this fairy story a happy ending.) It is one of these pavilions, Le Pavillon de Levant, that Kenyon Kramer today calls home.

Gatehouses, of course, were never designed to be especially commodious, and this one is no exception. Before Kenyon added some practical essentials – of which more later – the pavilion consisted of a salon and hall on the ground floor with a pair of bedrooms above, the floors linked in one corner by a narrow mahogany spiral staircase. Small as the house was, it had one great advantage over equally tiny but more modern buildings in that its proportions, although miniature in scale, could not be bettered. As Kenyon says, 'It is the perfect cube, and therefore supremely comfortable to be in; because the proportions are good, you feel good in the space.'

It is an oft-repeated rule of good decorating that the smaller the space, the larger the scale of the furnishings and the decoration should be. Following this maxim, Kenyon decided to use the boldest of prints throughout, starting with Braquenié's traditional 'Tree of Life' design as bed hangings and cover in the main bedroom. The mindset continues down through the rest of the house with an exuberant toile de Jouy, also by Braquenié. In the salon, it covers every surface to great effect. The subtle, all-over two-tone design, coupled with the sobering, softening tones of the pea green painted woodwork, gives the room a look of utter comfort and timelessness. The furniture, too, is hardly doll's house in scale. Everything is full-sized, including the Baldwin grand piano in the salon, but some subtle visual tricks have also been played. For example, instead of using sofas in the centre of the room, Kenyon has designed squashy, cushioned banquettes that sit neatly around the walls, covered in the ubiquitous toile.

The original pavilion was built without a kitchen. Mindful of the disparity between classical elegance and modern practicality, Kenyon designed a glazed lean-to kitchen with dark green glazing bars that, from above, could be taken for a perfectly in-period orangery. Away from the main preparation area, a garden room complete with traditional stove leads out to a courtyard. In the kitchen itself, a slate sink is set into a limestone worktop; in traditional Provençal fashion, the kitchen equipment is stored on shelves beneath the worktop, hidden by striped linen curtains. The table, which also has a stone top, was specially made to fit the space (*previous spread and right*).

But to return to the aforementioned practicalities, as Kenyon says, 'I'm an American – I need my kitchen and my bathroom.' But how to incorporate them both into the period design without disturbing the classical symmetry inside and, equally importantly, outside, too? The bathroom proved to be relatively simple. Kenyon carved out a suitable space from what was already there: 'I cut a hole, almost an oval, from an existing dressing room.' This is now a cabin-like space complete with both a shower and a chic bathtub panelled in deepest mahogany.

The kitchen presented more of a problem. Impossible to incorporate within the existing fabric, it would require the building of an extension. Kenyon's solution was worthy of a 17th-century classical architect. Aware that any extension could be seen, and found wanting, from the upper floors of the main house, he designed the lean-to kitchen with a glass roof, the whole inspired by orangeries of the period. All that can be seen from above are the dark green glazing bars, with presumably the suggestion of potted lemon and orange trees within.

Now the work is finished, Kenyon is a happy man. 'It is the perfect house. Everyone who visits wants it; because the scale is so good, you feel good, and know this is how you want to live.'

Kenyon has pursued the same principles upstairs as on the ground floor. There are two bedrooms and a minuscule bathroom, carved from an existing dressing room to make an almost cabin-like space. Although not every wall is covered in toile – in the main bedroom, because the walls slope steeply, Kenyon decided to paint them a pale terracotta as a foil for the dramatic toile-draped period *lit bateau* – the overall principle remains one of larger-than-life scale for a smaller-than-usual space. This is epitomized by the choice of bed as well as the other, rather masculine pieces of furniture (*opposite and this page*).

ON THE RAMPARTS

Light-filled, calm, gentle: soothing adjectives all – and all of which accurately describe the French home of the Hill family, built on the ramparts of old Mougins, in the hills behind Nice. The ramparts are circular, as befits a fortified village, so the house is actually curved, following the lines of the wall.

Jean and her late husband Douglas Hill, who already owned an antique shop in Mougins called French Country Living, bought the house some years ago. They and their two daughters transformed the interior so that it now has as much charm as the ancient exterior.

When the family found the house, having searched the area for many years, it had had the same owner for four decades. Decorated in the 1950s, it was clearly in need of change. Although they could see that much work would have to be done, in the event they had to do far more than they had ever imagined.

After the restoration work had begun, the Hills found that the roof terrace, erected many years earlier, had over time pushed the house downwards and outwards to such an extent that the whole house needed underpinning. Every floor had to come down and the entire house basically reinstated using concrete and steel. This drastic rebuilding did have its compensations. Once the house was gutted, they were able to appreciate the essential simplicity of the space – especially since, in its former incarnation, one room was bright blue and another bright green.

A 19th-century armoire, fitted with glazed panels rather than chicken wire or fabric, is used to store dishes, pots, bottles and jars (*left*). A traditional hexagonal tiled floor, striped cotton curtains, a comfortable daybed dressed in linen and a charming antique painted panel above – perfect French style (*opposite*).

The builders carried out a great feat of engineering, including rendering the house absolutely waterproof from the horizontal sheets of rain that sometimes lash the area. The work took 18 months, and the result was just what they wanted – a house that is very much of the true South of France; neither glittery nor flashy, but cool, comfortable and imbued with the spirit of the locality. After the dramatic house surgery, very little of the original fabric remained, with the exception of some ceiling beams, but the Hills were anxious to achieve a sense of timeless unity, understanding that in this type and age of house, you don't dictate to the house – the house dictates to you and tells you what you should do, as in laying simple flooring throughout, for example.

The choice of such flooring is all one pattern of reclaimed hexagonal terracotta tiles, which are typical of the region. They opted for simple wall treatments, too. There is not a straight wall in the house; the plasterwork followed the stone walls, which are themselves curved. The curved wall surface was also far from smooth; the traditional method is to attach chicken wire to the stone before plastering so that the plaster adheres to the wire rather than slipping off the stone, which is a completely different technique and so gives the walls a completely different texture. When it came to choosing the colour for the textural walls, the clarity of the light in this part of the country determined the palette that the Hills chose – such as the varying soft shades of ochre, which they built up in tonal layers.

In the drawing room, a late 18th-century pier mirror, inset into a carved and gilded boiserie panel, surmounts a decorated 18th-century Italian console table. On one side of the English Chesterfield sofa (piled with cushions made from the monogrammed panels of old linen sheets) is a fine Louis XIV bookcase, replete with more carving and subtle decoration (*previous spread*).

Endlessly adaptable and always attractive, the armoire is a staple of French country furniture. Here, the Hills converted a 19th-century Directoire-style bookcase into an armoire for storing and displaying their collection of ceramics and glass. Many of the pieces are traditional regional designs and distinctive earth-toned glazes, a number of which are still produced today in potteries around the countryside (*far left and left*).

In another bedroom is a traditional French colonial iron bed, dating from the 19th century, complete with a curved metal frame; delicate, unlined white curtains are tied in knots along its length. Cushions are made from old pieces of French toile, part of the Hills' collection of textiles. At one side of the room is an imposing 18th-century Swedish painted *buffet à deux corps* (*above and opposite*).

WHEN IT CAME TO CHOOSING THE COLOUR FOR THE WALLS, THE CLARITY OF THE LIGHT IN THIS PART OF THE COUNTRY DETERMINED THE PALETTE THAT THE HILLS CHOSE – SUCH AS ALL THE VARYING SOFT SHADES OF OCHRE, WHICH THEY BUILT UP IN TONAL LAYERS.

A 19th-century white wrought-iron bed is matched with an unusual 18th-century Swedish commode and, above it, an elegant gilded mirror (*opposite*). Other original pieces include this forged-iron painted bench from the 19th century, with cushions made from old blue and white textiles (*left*). Dating from the late 18th century, this chair, piled with more toile-covered cushions, still has its original rush seat (*below*).

As for furnishing this singular house, the Hills indulged their love of the 18th century, looking for a mixture of French and Italian pieces, which is appropriate to this part of France; they also like a mixture of painted furniture and fruitwoods, realizing that each style complements the other. There is but one piece of English furniture in the entire house – an early Chesterfield sofa, which sits very happily beside its more southerly neighbours. The whole family shares a love of old textures and textiles. And wherever they could they covered the chairs with old, sometimes dyed, linen. Patterns, too, were mixed together – stripes, checks and toiles, sometimes combined with floral designs.

From the windows, the green slopes of Cap Ferrat and the Mediterranean beyond can always be seen – a pleasure at any time of year, bathed as they are in the unique Provençal light. It is a lovely house and, rightly, much loved by all the family.

SPARE SOPHISTICATION

A peasant's house outside Grasse, dating from the 17th century, was restored by the late antique dealer Maurizio Epifani. 'Old houses should be left in their original state as far as possible,' he said, 'and there should never be heavy restructuring of the exterior, which should remain integral to the surrounding environment.'

The late Maurizio Epifani opened L'Oro dei Farlocchi, his antique shop in Milan, many years ago, when antique collecting and selling were still both traditional and conventional. Imagine, therefore, customers' surprise at a shop filled with fruit machines and 1950s robots next to antique Chinese chairs and Provençal armoires. The idea was, he says, to stock the 'improbable and the unlikely', and its success was both immediate and lasting.

So it is surprising that the house Maurizio bought in Provence, near Grasse, was minimal in style, with a sense of space and light that seemed in complete contrast to his shop. Although this area has been well populated since the 19th century, when Grasse became the heart of the French perfume industry, it was once as sparsely inhabited as the rest of rural Provence. Maurizio's house – its core at any rate – dates from the 17th century and was the home of a peasant family who worked the land for the principal landowning family of the district. Unsurprisingly, over the centuries, various additions and alterations had been made – so much so that, by the time Maurizio bought it, he felt there was little major work to be done.

The garden design and the choice of plants are as important as the arrangement of the rooms. As well as olive trees, *Arbutus unedo* and a grape vine growing up the front of the house, there is an airy pergola supporting kiwi fruit vines (*opposite and above*).

Looking towards a swimming pool designed in classical style, with a raised edge like a formal canal. Behind the pool is a stag at rest, set against a backdrop of greenery, almost as if he were alive (*right*).

Maurizio Epifani restored this former farmworker's dwelling with as light a hand as possible. In the airy living room, for example, there is comfort, there is style and there is also simplicity. Well-upholstered chairs and sofas sit next to choice 18th-century pieces. Both walls and upholstery are neutral in tone, enlivened with cushions made from old textiles and the odd galloping horse (*opposite and right*).

With his cultivated eye for the old and the antique, Maurizio always felt strongly that the essence of the house should stay relatively intact. Equally crucial was not to try to change the house's character; it should remain in feeling as it was originally designed – or, as Maurizio put it, 'Don't try to transform a country house into a castle.' With this in mind, he tried to do minimal work on the interior. The main changes were installing a staircase to link the upper-floor living room with the garden and the addition of two bathrooms.

Inside, the house is almost austere in its simplicity. Each room is painted in the softest of whites and there is little contrast. Beams and woodwork are painted in the same colours as the walls, and the floors have neutral coverings. The blank canvas allowed him to include interesting pieces of furniture, much of it from the 18th century: 'poor French furniture', as he called it – that is, simple country pieces as opposed to grand antiques. Against this background he added flashes of colour and unusual details, as in the living room, where the windows are flanked by antique waxed wooden pilasters rather than curtains. These same windows are surmounted by a prancing wooden horse, one of the 'animalier' objects he collected.

This is all in accord with his views on how the interiors of old houses should be treated: 'For the interior, if it has to be refurbished, old materials only should be used, or – if that is not possible – materials that are as similar as possible to the original, such as recycled old wooden flooring, old stone, old fireplaces and so on.' Textiles also came within this strict remit. They were to be thick linens, often old and second-hand, and in natural colours – beiges, dusty blues, faded greens and 'always, always white'. Simplicity was important to Maurizio: 'Never be excessive with the decoration. Too many fabrics are detrimental – curtains and bedspreads with heavy patterns, florals, little *ton-sur-ton* sets.' An overload of pattern can make an otherwise plain interior seem fussy, and in a hot climate it is essential that the inside the house is as cool and quiet as possible.

AN OVERLOAD OF PATTERN CAN MAKE AN OTHERWISE
PLAIN INTERIOR SEEM FUSSY, AND IN A HOT
CLIMATE IT IS ESSENTIAL THAT THE INSIDE OF THE
HOUSE IS AS COOL AND QUIET AS POSSIBLE.

In the principal bedroom, there is little in the way of fabrics other than a heavy antique quilt on a bed dressed with white linen. The requisite 'animalier' element takes the form of a large painting of an elk propped against the wall (*far left*). The adjoining bathroom features a double wooden washstand, set with two basins and lit, unexpectedly, with a table lamp at each end of the upper shelf (*above*). The bathtub is positioned near the shuttered window (*left*).

The kitchen is as light and airy as one could wish – white on white, with the witty touch of a ceramic, glazed bas-relief of a full-grown olive tree growing across the wall (*opposite*). If you live in Provence and have the space, it is always worth having both an outdoor and an indoor dining room. The latter is useful not only when it is too cold but also when it is too hot. The dining room in this house is conscious of its past incarnation, being a restored lean-to with a full-length cupboard for crockery, wide window openings carved out of the walls and a sloping beamed ceiling painted white (*this page*).

The kitchen is as simple as the drawing room – once again, it is all white, and the central decorative motif is a subtle white ceramic rendition of an olive tree, which grows upwards, spreading its branches and leaves over the wall.

Garden life is important here. The indoor dining room is surrounded by greenery, while the outside dining area is a long terrace running down one side of the house. When Maurizio bought the house, the swimming pool was already in place, as well as an additional wing, which he made into a guest house. He explained that he had not done much to that area 'other than refresh it, lightening the surroundings and adding the bronze deer to overlook the pool'. The landscape designer Stefano Baccari was enlisted to 'modify' the rest of the garden, refining the plant and vegetative life to exclude species that are not native to the area.

The final result is a charming combination of the simple and the sophisticated, with something to look at at every turn – very similar, perhaps, to the sensation felt by those early collectors at L'Oro dei Farlocchi.

All sunshine houses need shady, outdoor areas where comfortable seating and cool drinks beckon. Here, wicker armchairs are set beneath a loggia at one end of the house. Designed in the form of a rough-hewn pergola, it features massive beams that provide support to climbing plants and shrubs (*right*).

CALM AND COOL

The ancient house that Nelly Guyot owns in Ramatuelle, and the way
that she has updated it, is a textbook example of how to achieve the right
look – the right look, that is, for a simple yet comfortable summer life.

If you decided to follow, in a general sort of way, the
guidance implicitly offered by Nelly Guyot, with barely any
effort at all, you, too, could have the ideal holiday house:
a place that is cool and calm to live in, ageless and with
perfect style. And even if your own particular haven does
not look quite as flawless as Nelly's house, it will still be
a very pleasant place in which to live.

But to begin at the beginning. Some years ago,
Nelly Guyot, Parisian interior designer and lover of the
simple style, decided to buy a house in the Provençal
village of Ramatuelle. This is a popular village for good
reason – it combines both the virtues and beauty of the
archetypal fortified medieval hillside village with the more
temporal pleasures of beach and town life in the port of
St Tropez below. Nelly came to Ramatuelle in search of
a traditional *maison de village* – a style that has long been
popular for holiday houses, since it is both full of character
and yet small enough to be easily cared for. But for Nelly,
a single house would have been too small for her needs,
so she bought two adjoining houses, dating back to at least
the 17th century, and converted them into one.

An original stone fireplace is flanked by a cushioned stone
seat, an English armchair, a small African chair and a low
coffee table (*opposite*). An unlikely mixture of objects –
including a processional lamp, a Moroccan mirror and
a Greek bust – make a harmonious whole (*right*).

The outdoor dining area (*right*). Beside the stairs is an old, closed French armoire, originally made in two parts for ease of transport (*below*). The kitchen is a traditional but with quirky details such as the wall lights, which date from the Empire period. The sink area is surrounded by black tiles, called *anciennes de Salerne*, made in the town of Salerne, the centre of Provençal tile making. An old farm table, a 20th-century metal chair from Italy and a collection of 19th-century terracotta and glass complete the picture (*opposite*).

Apart from giving her more space, this arrangement meant that Nelly was able to configure the rooms in a way that suited her needs. As it transpired, she didn't need to alter a great deal. Houses of this age have their own pace and character, and are all the better when that is respected.

There were some obvious things to be done: two houses meant two kitchens, so she made the smaller one into a study, and embellished and enlarged the other. The main reception room opens onto the terrace and is now *un espace vivant* – a living space. Much of the restoration and repair work that was carried out was utilitarian and practical, such as introducing new windows and installing different stairs. It was, as she says, 'a lot of work to achieve the simple'. Thus much of the work now appears invisible, but that is what good design and decoration is all about: the amount of work you put in to achieve the unseen and unnoticed; the work that underpins the foundations, whether literal or metaphorical, is what informs and dictates the final design.

Once the basic remedial work had been completed, says Nelly, the essential thing was to continue to respect the style of the house and ensure the decoration complemented the

architecture. For her, this is not difficult. Her signature is purity of line, and in everything she does a certain aesthetic prevails – not severe exactly, but certainly one without excessive frills or furbelows. For example, the entire house is decorated in a pared-down neutral palette, the better to offset the heat of a Mediterranean summer's day. She uses white and more white, different shades of the base colour, sometimes softened with a little cream, occasionally with a little added grey and sometimes yellow – what Nelly calls 'couleurs claires', which are very different from the colours that she would use in an urban decorative scheme.

HOUSES OF THIS AGE HAVE THEIR OWN PACE AND CHARACTER. ONE MUST 'RESPECT THE STYLE OF THE HOUSE', SAYS NELLY.

A Catalan table, a metal chair and a military folding seat furnish this comfortable sitting room, once a shelter for sheep; the tapestry cushions are from Chelsea Textiles (*this spread*).

EVERYTHING NELLY DOES, FROM COLOUR TO CURTAINS, IS INTENDED TO PRODUCE A HOUSE THAT IS BOTH A REFUGE AND A DELIGHT, AND WHICH WORKS PERFECTLY.

Nothing is quite as it seems in this room. Against the large mirror on the floor – designed as an overmantel mirror – is a 20th-century mirrored commode, known as a *meuble de chemise*, while the elegant metal chair is, in fact, the frame of a 19th-century chair, which would normally have been upholstered (*left*). Nelly has sought to achieve harmony of tone in every room in the house. Here, the painted chair with its rush seat, the painted wooden table and the antique paper-covered box are all of a piece (*above*).

The furniture was bought by Nelly specifically for this project. It is all old – her preferred style – and follows the rule of simplicity of look and line; some of it is in good condition, some not. Many of the pieces are painted in soft greys and whites, several of them then decorated by Nelly. She also bought local Provençal dishes and glassware that would be in keeping with the furniture; they are pieces that can be used every day, including chunky, glazed earthenware and thick, generous glasses – immensely practical as well as good-looking, and made to the same designs for hundreds of years.

When it came to the choice of textiles, someone with such a strong preference for simplicity would have been most unlikely to introduce exotic brocades and printed silks into the decorative scheme. And so it is – plain fabrics or stripes are all that have been allowed. Whether on beds or curtains, cushions or covers, no glimmer of a print or intricate weave is to be seen.

What this adds up to is a textbook lesson in decorating. Nelly Guyot does not deviate from what she sets out to do; she understands the limitations as well as the possibilities of a space. Everything she does, from colour to curtains, is both designed to and succeeds in creating a house that is a refuge and a delight.

Another simple bedroom is dominated by a 17th-century armoire, which was restored by Nelly to its original beauty. The wall light is converted from a 1940s ceiling light, and the bedside light is an old church candlestick converted to electricity. A door opens onto the adjoining bathroom (*above and opposite*).

A Sicilian frame of iron, both wrought and gilded, adds splendour to a bed covered in a spread of traditional *courte-pointe* (*opposite*). Showing the charm of simplicity, the beds in this twin room are folding military camp beds, while the mattresses are new, made of wool and covered in cotton and silk. The small red bear is from Russia (*this page*).

PERFECT IN PINK

For Enrica Stabile, it was love at first sight. The house at Le Thor was exactly her idea of what a Provençal farmhouse should be: a perfect limewashed rectangle, with an old well in the front, two shady plane trees and, on either side of the building, broad fields bright with poppies and golden sunflowers.

The Italian designer Enrica Stabile bought her farmhouse at Le Thor, near Avignon, many years ago – at a time, as she puts it, 'before Peter Mayle' (the writer whose bestselling books popularized Provence) and when prices were much lower. The sundial on an outside wall gives the date of the building as 1870, and when she first saw it, it was in a dilapidated state – 'more ruin than house' – but she was immediately smitten with it, to the bewilderment of her loved ones.

'When I called my family to say that I was buying a house, they thought me completely mad. They said they would never come, and I would have to do everything myself.' So she did. 'That first year was very difficult. As with many old farmhouses, the animals had been housed downstairs along with the hay and the agricultural machinery.

The old farmhouse's pleasing lines will appeal to every lover of rural France. Restoring it meant also giving it back its pride; the façade is a soft limewashed pink with white shutters, and a paved and gravelled terrace runs the length of the house, flanked by square terracotta pots and edged with box (*this page and opposite*).

PERFECT IN PINK 107

Upstairs had been lived in, but it was all very primitive. It needed major work. The roof was replaced, the windows repositioned and I had to create entirely new bathrooms.'

But there is nothing a determined woman in love cannot achieve when she wants to, particularly if, like Enrica Stabile, she is already a successful antique dealer and interior decorator. The house today is very different from the ruin she first saw. Upstairs there are five bedrooms and three bathrooms. The bedrooms are mainly decorated in a rich buttery colour, the bathrooms in pink: 'It makes you look healthy, especially in the mornings.'

The charming garden room was once the space where tractors and other essential pieces of agricultural equipment were kept. Now, transformed by the addition of three tall French windows, it serves in winter as a semi-conservatory and in summer as a dining room for when the sun is too strong for outdoor dining (*opposite and this page*).

THE KITCHEN IS PACKED WITH DECORATIVE PIECES AS WELL
AS ALL THE THINGS NECESSARY FOR COOKING AND EATING.
IT IS MUCH LIVED IN – THE WHOLE FAMILY LOVES TO COOK.

Each bedroom has its own character and colour, and is filled with print and pattern used in ingenious and quirky ways. 'I have a passion for textiles. I come from the fashion world, so I love to use and mix them, and create subtle or startling effects according to the room and the season.'

Downstairs, on the ground floor, are a south-facing sitting room, a kitchen-dining room in what was once the stables and a small study complete with piano. There is also a wonderful garden room that was once the home of tractors and other agricultural essentials, where Enrica installed three tall French windows and now the space is used all year – in winter as a semi-conservatory, sheltering the more delicate plants and the lemon trees from the sometimes cruel weather; and in summer as a shaded dining room when it is too hot to sit outside. As so often in farmhouses, the kitchen, which incorporates a large dining area, is warm and welcoming, coloured in 'cream and green with touches of red; it sounds awful but it works'. It is packed with decorative pieces as well as all the things necessary for cooking and eating. It is much lived in – the whole family, including children and grandchildren, loves to cook, and, of course, everyone loves to eat.

The south-facing sitting room is another favourite spot – the decoration here was inspired by a striking pink and blue Murano glass chandelier.

The large, warm kitchen is more accurately described as a living room, incorporating as it does the functions of a dining space, as well as, elsewhere in the room, a pair of comfortable chairs to sit in and decorative objects to look at. Under an elaborate chandelier, a large, old trestle table is laid, with traditional garden chairs around it. A further table, this one more workaday, runs parallel to the cooking range and sink. Rugs mark out various areas, with different lighting in each space, and all the disparate items are pulled together by Enrica's colour-filled collections of everything from baskets to ceramics, glass and kitchenware (*opposite and above left*). Upstairs, a corridor leads to the bedrooms and bathrooms (*above right*).

Each of the five bedrooms is painted in pale, neutral tones, with the main decorative interest concentrated in the textiles. This predominantly blue room, for example, combines at least seven different patterns, all layered and used together on a pair of white-painted iron beds (*left*). Red is the main colour in this room, with not only checks of varying sizes but also floral borders and antique red and white cushions. The effect is softened with lush swags of white muslin, draped in deep folds the length of the bed. Muslin curtains hang beneath a soft, scalloped, red and white check pelmet (*above and opposite*).

This was given to Enrica by her husband as an olive branch after she went ahead and bought the house. The family's initial disapproval and unwillingness to join in the project has of course dispersed but, as Enrica remarks, 'Now the house is beautiful and comfortable, they all adore it – and even help in the garden. As I remind them, they are very welcome but they are just my beloved guests.'

Enrica understands the art of arrangement, and each corner holds a combination of objects, flowers and furniture. 'As far as furniture goes, I was actually lucky, as I didn't have anything apart from some nice things my husband gave me from a former family house, so I just

bought little by little through the years. I bought a few good pieces and many nice inexpensive things to make the house really warm and welcoming, as I spend as much time as I can here. I have never actually bought anything new, except the bidets and lavatories – so as not to disappoint my plumber completely.'

And now that the house is finished? 'I'm an antique dealer and a designer, so it has been a most rewarding job to do my own house in the way I liked best. Now that it's over, I feel pretty desperate and need a new challenge.' Given Enrica's determination and style, that challenge surely cannot be long in coming.

'I JUST BOUGHT LITTLE BY
LITTLE THROUGH THE YEARS –
A FEW GOOD PIECES AND MANY
NICE INEXPENSIVE THINGS TO
MAKE THE HOUSE REALLY WARM
AND WELCOMING.'

The bathrooms, with the exception of one broadly based blue one, are predominantly pink because, in Enrica's opinion, pink makes you look healthy, especially in the mornings. Whether blue or pink, though, her bathrooms are decorated with a judicious mix of the pretty and the practical. The main features are large, old bathtubs and basins – she prefers never to buy new, although she made a concession to her plumber with the lavatories and bidets. There are also decorative plates on the walls, embroidered vintage towels and antique mirrors and lights. As elsewhere in the house, there are flower-filled glasses and jugs/pitchers everywhere you look (*opposite and this page*).

DECORATIVE DELIGHTS

When Jocelyne and Jean-Louis Sibuet saw the location of what is now the Villa Marie – on a sloping hill outside the village of Ramatuelle, with views across vineyards on one side and down to the Mediterranean on the other – they could not resist the opportunity to bring yet another old building back to life.

Jocelyne and Jean-Louis Sibuet are from France's Savoie region – a part of the country that has much in common with rural Provence, especially in the appreciation and understanding of artisanal skills and objects. The Sibuets still live in the Savoie – in Megève – and it was there where they first channelled their talents into transforming old, vernacular buildings into small hotels of great charm and individuality.

They began with a mountain lodge, Au Coin du Feu, followed by Les Fermes de Marie, where they turned several farmhouses into a small *hameau* of comfort and delight. After several more restorations in Megève, the Sibuets went to Lyons, where they transformed four 15th- and 16th-century town houses into Cour des Loges, and then south to Provence, where they bought an old farmhouse and turned it into La Bastide de Marie. Unsurprisingly, Provence exerted its allure on the Sibuets. Although they were not originally looking for anywhere on the coast, when they saw the location of what is now the Villa Marie, they could not resist the temptation to begin a new adventure.

Archways and open doors lead the eyes – and the feet – into the gardens, and to the views of the landscape beyond (*right*).

If a sea view through a grove of umbrella pines is your idea of a true Provençal retreat, then nothing could be more perfect than the Villa Marie. Set on a hill above St Tropez, this old farmhouse, now a hotel, has been completely restored, while the land surrounding it has been transformed from scrub into a paradise of cypress and citrus, jasmine and roses (*left and above*).

What is unusual, if not exceptional, about Jocelyne and Jean-Louis Sibuet is that, although the Villa Marie was their seventh project, every hotel that they have done has the feel of a private house – a large house, to be sure, but a house and a home nevertheless. This is not accidental, but a considered strategy: 'I treat each new hotel exactly as if it were my own second home,' says Jocelyne.

It is also due in large part to the fact that the pair's creative talents complement each other in a remarkable and highly felicitous way. Jean-Louis is master of the broad brushstrokes – the buildings and the landscape – while Jocelyne is queen of the finer details – the colours, the textiles, the look of the thing. They are both interested in old furniture, however. A decorator and a designer with an interest in common is surely a perfect match.

The gardens are linked to the interior by airy corridors and hallways, furnished with pieces that work both inside and out (*left*). The once untamed trees and shrubs have been tamed by Jean-Louis and, with the addition of many new indigenous plants, fashioned into a natural landscape that adds beauty to the estate (*below and opposite*).

The initial plan with Villa Marie was to renovate the old house while adding new buildings to accommodate a bar, restaurants and a spa, which would come under the umbrella of the original building; they would also landscape the terrain and build a swimming pool that was outstanding and yet in keeping with the setting.

Colour and colouring both inside and out were all important. In this part of Provence, colours are easily drained by the intense, strong light as well as by the reflection of the bright blue sea and sky. This means that, to be successful, colour schemes should either be in calm and pale, neutral-based tones or in shades that can stand up to the natural competition without leaving an impression of clashing tumult.

The Sibuets have solved the problem by embracing both options. The façade is deep ochre, with a traditional terracotta-tiled roof; inside, some equally strong colours can be found, but they relate closely to the earth colours of the Mediterranean – ochre, sienna and terracotta, used in conjunction with cool neutral shades of stone, cream and white. Earth tones are also found in surprising partnerships and unusual combinations, some astringent and some warm, such as rose, mauve as well as a soft, cool green.

These latter colours are not normally found in this part of the world, nor are they colours that normally grace hotel rooms, no matter how personal the touch; but Jocelyne Sibuet is a natural decorator, and she has the natural decorator's gift of mixing the unusual with the ordinary to produce something new and totally fresh.

There are around 40 bedrooms at Villa Marie and each one has been decorated in its own, highly individual way. Furniture is as important a part of the decorative scheme as the chosen colours, and neither Jocelyne nor Jean-Louis would ever go down the 'contract hotel' route. Their love of old furniture can be seen throughout the hotel – Jean-Louis, in particular, has always collected old pieces, both French and Italian.

Standing on an old terracotta floor in the hallway is an imposing wooden console table, flanked by a pair of antique chairs and used to display a collection of shells, driftwood and bleached coral (*left*). Shells and other natural finds are an integral part of the decoration at Villa Marie, which delights in creating compositions on every available surface. Here, a carved wooden table is used to display a collection of antique candle holders, combined with domed glass jars filled with shells, a stone urn overflowing with ivy and a pair of ceramic doves (*above*).

For Villa Marie, the Sibuets found any number of Provençal pieces, both painted and made in fruitwood, to which they have added decorative bits found in local brocantes as well as a few contemporary items, all combined to make a thoroughly original mélange. The finds are scattered through the building accentuated by a collection of natural and sometimes eccentric objects: on an ornate table in a hallway, coral and seashells are arranged as sculptural forms, and around the bar are hundreds of seashells glued into place by Jean-Louis in an arrangement that is both charming and evocative of an earlier era on the French Riviera.

The bedrooms are simple in concept, with beamed ceilings and wrought-iron bedsteads; the combination of walls and furnishings keeps the spaces cool while reflecting the light and scents of Provence. Bathrooms open directly off the bedrooms or are located within the bedrooms themselves. As elsewhere in the hotel, natural fabrics reign supreme – curtains and cushions are in linen, silk or cotton, striped and plain, informal and subtle.

The outside, once scrubland, has been tamed by Jean-Louis to make the perfect, rambling Mediterranean garden, with pathways through the pine trees, and the whole area was planted with more than 3,000 new plants and trees, from palms and cypress to tamarisk and lavender. This rural landscape is crowned with a swimming pool that was carved out of the rocky ground around the house and now seems to be part of the natural terrain.

The effect conveyed by Villa Marie is one of careless ease – a testament to the theory that the more effort you put into a project, the more effortless it will appear to others.

Each bedroom is decorated in a completely contemporary way, incorporating a mix of antique furniture and modern decorative objects and textiles. Colour schemes are based on the Provençal palette but softened. In this room, the soft bleached green of the summer is paired with a deep aubergine, the latter shade apparent in the carefully delineated flower motif that can be seen on curtains and cushions. The stone urns – a recurring theme throughout the house – here serve as bedside lights and, as elsewhere at Villa Marie, the outdoor world is not far away. Through French windows, a balustraded terrace beckons (*above*).

Design of the bathrooms is an important part of the overall concept at Villa Marie, and many are within the bedrooms themselves – placed not at the far side of the room, but near the entrance. Here a freestanding tub is flanked by a pair of bowl-shaped basins, which look almost as if they have been carved from the rock outside (*right*). Unlined linen adorns the bed in this simple bedroom. At the window, which leads onto an ochre-painted balcony, the curtains are a soft honey and white – colours taken from the Provençal countryside (*below*).

THE RURAL LANDSCAPE, WHICH
WAS PLANTED WITH MORE THAN
3,000 NEW PLANTS AND TREES,
IS CROWNED WITH A SWIMMING
POOL THAT WAS CARVED OUT
OF THE ROCKY GROUND
AROUND THE HOUSE AND
NOW SEEMS PART OF THE
NATURAL TERRAIN.

Even the swimming pool appears to have happened
almost by chance. It has been designed to incorporate
a stony outcrop, which has become an integral part
of the pool itself. On one side, a waterfall tumbles
into the water; on the other, a wooden deck has been
erected that faces down to the sea. Neighbouring
pines and clumps of wild rosemary and thyme scent
the air around (*left and above*).

The kitchen has been recreated from what was almost a ruin – a fact that would be hard to divine from what is now a beautifully furnished and decorated room. From the 19th-century zinc-topped wine taster's table to the decorative panel of antique metal whisks that hangs above the marble sinks, the furniture was all found by Martine Delaune, often with the help of decorator Daisy Simon, in antique shops and brocantes throughout Provence. It was then combined with modern equipment such as the efficient cooking range and the practical hanging metal utensils rack (designed by Daisy Simon) for the Delaunes' collection of copper pans (*opposite, this page and overleaf*).

CLASSICAL RESTORATION

Like so many other country houses – particularly in the large rural areas of France – the fortunes of this renovated bastide took a turn for the worse in the 19th century, when it slowly degenerated from being an elegant 18th-century mansion into a lowly farm with gardens levelled and turned into fields.

There is a particular kind of classical French country house that exudes tranquillity and calm – a house that has apparently stood unaltered for many years or even centuries, settled and secure in its own surroundings.

This is the impression given by the Delaune family's bastide outside Aix-en-Provence: a fairy-tale mansion complete with hipped tower, immaculate gardens, an ornamental potager, a real swan lake and numerous beautiful trees, all apparently cared for by generations of talented gardeners. Inside, large cool rooms, subtly coloured walls and comfortable antique furniture on floors of ancient terracotta tiles glowing with the patina of years – all speak of a life of unbroken harmony.

The reality, though, is different. When Christian and Martine Delaune bought the bastide in 1999, it was a ruined farm with small, partition-walled rooms, false ceilings and crumbling beams, flanked by untended fields and pasture. Its attractions, on the other hand, included its size – lots of space for their four children – and its abundance of land.

Also, to their delight, there were several mature trees surviving in what remained of the original gardens. Although the house was in a state of bad disrepair when the Delaunes found it, its history was one of vibrant life. Built in the 18th century, it had once been a grand house, with elaborately frescoed ceilings and even more elaborately planted gardens.

The couple had searched for two years before finding their crumbling manor; in that time, Martine collected decorative ideas from books and magazines so that, when they eventually bought the house, she had a good idea of how she wanted it to look. After removing the partition walls, false ceilings and other 20th-century additions and detractions, they set about returning the house as nearly as possible to its original design.

Fireplaces had been closed up, windows altered, the layout of rooms changed and, with little archival information, Christian and Martine had to rely to a degree on intelligent guesswork. It took 12 months to restore the house – a short enough time, you might think, but at certain periods there were as many as 70 workers on site at the same time.

The discipline and purity of line that underwrites the Delaune decorating style can be seen to detailed effect in this composition of painted side table and mirror, where every object has been picked for its part in the greater whole (*above*). The painted dining table at one end of the kitchen, designed and made by Daisy Simon, works well with the early 20th-century painted chairs. The tall French windows open onto a vegetable garden, one of the areas that Christian Delaune has painstakingly restored (*opposite*).

ALTHOUGH THE HOUSE WAS IN A STATE OF BAD DISREPAIR WHEN THE DELAUNES FOUND IT, ITS HISTORY WAS ONE OF VIBRANT LIFE. THE RESULT OF THE RESTORATION IS A TRIUMPH.

When the Delaunes had almost finished reviving the heart of the house, they brought in interior decorator Daisy Simon, based in Aix, to help them to find the right furniture and fittings for the place. With her, they travelled around Provence visiting brocantes and towns such as L'Isle-sur-la-Sorgue and Aix itself, until they had found enough distinctive pieces for every room.

It was important that their finds should be elegant but not over-elaborate, since the Delaunes had taken care to retain the spirit of the original, simple architecture. The floors of hexagonal terracotta tiles remained uneven; the walls retained their rough texture and were painted – both exterior and interior – with limewash in the traditional manner. As seen on these pages, the result of the restoration is a triumph: a house that really does now exude peace and calm – even if it has only been in that happy state for relatively few years.

The drawing room is yet another achievement, seemingly imbued with the permanence of age, but in fact made from what had been a warren of partition-walled spaces, false ceilings and bricked-up windows (*this page*). Every bed in the house, including this daybed, has been painted in chalk-based paints and dressed in white linen; simplicity is the intention and result (*right*).

One of the pleasures of the restoration is the way in which the owners have retained the 'imperfect' structure of the original house and combined it with modern stylishness. Upstairs, for example, they have used such integral elements as the uneven and beautiful old terracotta floor tiles and the heavy ceiling beams as a background to their subtle and delicate brand of interior decoration, where beds are made with pristine white linen, draped with filmy fabric and painted in off-white neutral colours. The result, in both the bedrooms and bathrooms, is a natural and gentle effect that is also remarkably individual and surprisingly practical (*far left, above and left*).

The combined kitchen and dining room extends across one part of the ground floor; at each end is a door opening into a courtyard. The room is simple in the extreme and, as usual in this house, colour is the defining element of the decoration (*opposite*). Colour has been used throughout the house to create a series of artistic compositions. In this corner, no other element is needed to complement the green-painted cupboard door, the blue-washed door and the terracotta walls (*below*).

AN ARTISTIC MASTERCLASS

Of all the many beautiful areas in Provence, one of the most evocative is the ancient city of Arles and the strange, often wild countryside that surrounds it. The quality of the light there – so much admired by, among others, Vincent Van Gogh – seems even more luminous and clear than elsewhere in Provence.

The area around Arles is the province of artists, which is perhaps why the late Irene Silvagni and her film producer husband Giorgio lived there. Their house – a solid, rambling bastide – is hidden away in a village outside the city, where the air is warm and the trees are dense. Giorgio was also a talented artist and over time he and Irene transformed this old house into a place of surprises, where colour is not only a decorating device or space divider but a central character in the drama of the decoration. Around every corner is something unexpected. Yet to the Silvagnis there was a logical pattern; everything is there for a reason, and nothing is necessarily the same for ever.

Through the main entrance is a living hall, created from what was once a courtyard, with an oversized fireplace and seats layered in old textiles. Half cobbled and half paved, its plaster walls coloured and distressed in deep tones of red, the hall has an almost medieval appearance. By contrast, the kitchen-dining room on the other side of the house has a more domestic aspect with a door at either end opening onto cool courtyards.

The Silvagnis collected both new and old pottery made in Vallauris, and they used and displayed it constantly. The rubbed terracotta walls act as a fine backdrop for the pottery as well as for the painted table and chairs. Quirky touches include the wall-hung, wrought-iron table – made by Giorgio – that began life as an ornamental balcony in Spain before being hammered into its present form (*left and opposite*).

FURNITURE IS, ON THE WHOLE, SOLID AND REASSURING – CHOSEN TO SUIT BOTH THE HOUSE AND THE RURAL SURROUNDINGS.

Upstairs, tall windows with unlined, lightweight curtains let in the breezes, while thick walls keep out the heat. The master bedroom is especially cool, in both senses of the word – as dramatic as the rooms downstairs, with bold paint effects on walls and furniture – but also extremely comfortable, with an upholstered headboard draped in an old quilt and another quilt covering an inviting chair. The mosquito net here has been dyed blue, and in another bedroom a white one is hung from the ceiling behind the bed, like a classical coronet canopy. Along the upper floor, a landing leads to other rooms, many arranged enfilade.

Every room in the house is coloured in its totality so that it is truly an artist's creation, taking in every decorative element from the walls to the furniture to the textiles. In one room, for example, a wall is painted in deep blue and white stripes, and an armoire against the wall has been incorporated into the scheme, with its wood divides painted white and panels lined with bright red fabric as a contrast to the surrounding walls. Perhaps inspired by the Silvagnis' collection of green-glazed Vallauris pottery, a store cupboard against a terracotta-coloured wall in the dining end of the kitchen has been painted a warm lime-olive green, while the outside door has been painted blue. Again, the whole scheme exhibits a masterly use of traditional colours and techniques, all put together in a completely original way.

HALF COBBLED AND HALF PAVED, ITS PLASTER
WALLS COLOURED AND DISTRESSED IN DEEP VIBRANT
TONES OF RED, THE ENTRANCE HALL HAS AN
ALMOST MEDIEVAL APPEARANCE.

Against a wash of deep red plaster, the
imposing chimney piece in the hall – once
part of an outer courtyard – is garlanded
with Bargello-like tapestry pieces and crowned
with a striking stone pediment. More textile
remnants are piled in a basket next to the fire
(*left*). On one side of the room, a relatively
simple, late 18th-century bench seat has
been covered with a Provençal fabric and
draped with a quilted *boutis*. In the corner
is an oversized terracotta urn, reminiscent
of a water pot and subtly blending with the
red-toned plaster (*this page*).

As befits a true artist, Giorgio made his colours work hard. Not simply applied to the walls, they were layered, distressed, rubbed back and washed. Giorgio painted patterns over base colours, too – basic stripes, but also freehand designs, with flowers and leaves climbing over walls. Colour was also used to accentuate Irene's large and ever-increasing collection of textiles, which can be seen everywhere in the house – from the quilted *boutis* over beds, chairs, sofas and tables to the unusual hangings and small fragments of interestingly patterned cottons and silks used as cushions. Even the fireplace in the hall was draped with a couple of pieces of Bargello-like tapestry. Indeed, old textiles also made their way into the garden. Demonstrating a refreshing lack of respect for age or rarity, even the cushions scattered around the pool were covered in old fabric fragments.

Furniture is, on the whole, solid and reassuring – chosen to suit both the house and the surroundings. Unlike much of the furniture to be found in this part of France, the pieces are neither particularly Provençal nor particularly of a single period. The 20th century was as much admired in the Silvagni household as the 18th century, and country designs mix happily with more urban styles.

Like the rest of the house, the bathrooms have a raffish, eccentric charm. This one combines various periods and styles, incorporating heavy full-length curtains, an ornate gilded mirror, an old wooden washstand and a chrome and leather 1930s dressing stool (*above*). A slightly cooler, calmer atmosphere prevails on the upper floor – certainly along the corridors, where unlined curtains at the tall windows provide a shaded light while allowing the breeze to circulate through the bedrooms. One landing is graced by a pair of Italian woven leather chairs from the 1950s (*opposite*).

They are not precious, pampered pieces, but chosen to suit each particular room – and often painted with abandon to enter into the general scheme of things. There are quirky, unusual elements, too, which show the extent of the Silvagnis' imagination, such as the wrought-iron console table attached to the wall in the kitchen – which is, in fact, an old iron balcony found in a Spanish house, recycled and given a new life by Giorgio.

The garden is as mysterious as the house. Almost overgrown, with an air of being a hidden secret, it includes a swimming pool designed to look as if it had always been there and a dining table beneath a shady tree lit by a fantastical outdoor chandelier.

Nothing is expected, yet all is familiar and utterly comfortable – an effect that is difficult to achieve, and depended not only on Giorgio and Irene's decorative skills but also on their total understanding of the spirit of their beautiful old house.

Surprising yet also warm and comfortable colour palettes triumph in the bedroooms. The master bedroom is a harvest of damson, plum and grape, with a blue mosquito net. Leopard-print upholstered chairs add to the mix (*opposite*). Designed in 1929 by Mies van der Rohe and Lilly Reich, the famous Barcelona chair is suitable seating for the Roman emperor above (*above*). A bedroom carved from an old dovecote is an inviting sea of warm blues (*left*). As is typical in Provence, the Silvagnis treated the outside spaces as an extension of those indoors. Scattered around the garden are tables in sheltered spots, one overlit by an alfresco variation on the ceiling light. Another is set beneath a pergola with a split-cane hanging and a bench draped with textiles. The colours and patterns of the fabrics are echoed in the painted designs on the table itself (*overleaf*).

HAVEN OF PEACE

Life is fine in Ramatuelle, the medieval hill village above St Tropez, and many of the old houses here have been restored and transformed into doll's houses of delight. One of these belongs to Tita Bay, an Italian interior decorator, in whose hands it has become a doll's house of distinctive chic.

When looking at beautiful photographs of Provençal interiors, it is often hard to realize just how small many of the houses in Provence's medieval fortified villages really are. Take Ramatuelle, for instance, the old hill village above St Tropez. Many of the houses in the twisting, arcaded streets are tiny, with little more than one room on each floor, and lean up, as if for company, against the houses on either side.

In common with other fortified towns in the area, Ramatuelle was ravaged during the Middle Ages. It was fully reconstructed in 1620 after being destroyed in the Wars of Religion – but these days the only invading hordes are the relatively few tourists who have escaped from the crowded streets of St Tropez.

Village houses were not designed to have large gardens. The usual solution is a terrace – here a place of charm and comfort, with a bench that continues around the corner and is piled high with cushions in vintage fabrics. Pots of plants are everywhere, from oleander to geranium and verbena (*this page*). Cushions abound in the built-in seating area near the fireplace, and a comfortable chair, upholstered in stripes, is drawn up close to the fire (*opposite*).

THE ABSENCE OF ANY SENSE OF CLAUSTROPHOBIA IN THE TINY SPACE IS IN PART DUE TO TITA BAY'S SOPHISTICATED USE OF TEXTILES AND COLOURS.

It is in Ramatuelle that Tita Bay, an Italian interior decorator, has used her own particular doll's house to create a contemporary take on rustic Provençal style, using traditional elements in a highly untraditional way.

On the ground floor, entered from the street through a half-stable door, Tita has carved out separate spaces, each with a distinct role, which combine to make a most harmonious room. In the eating corner, by the window, is a round table covered in a floor-length cloth, while built-in cement seating, strewn with cushions, runs up to the oversized fireplace. The other side of the fireplace, where the seating continues along the wall, is a reading area, dominated by a comfortable chair drawn up to the hearth.

Tita uses textiles as punctuation points throughout the house. Both in her bedroom and in the living area, the tables are draped with full, floor-length cloths and the windows are dressed with voluminous, dramatic swathes of unlined fabric, which have been elaborately draped and tied in a way more often seen in high-ceilinged Parisian apartments.

A half-door, like a stable door, leads from the street into the main room of the house; although the overall space is small, it has been divided into distinct areas, and the eating area is on the street side (*opposite and this page*).

Striking old black and cream floor tiles unite various spaces in the house. Everything is drawn into the decorative scheme, including the stairs that lead down to the floor below; the retaining wall is used like a display table, and as a place for some of the many cushions that can be seen throughout the house. A trellis-fronted cupboard holds earthenware, and through the doorway can be seen Tita's bedroom with its elaborately draped curtains (*this page*). In the bedroom, fabric is everywhere – not only at the window, but also draped in voluminous folds over the table (*opposite*).

There are cushions everywhere – both inside and outside on her tiny flower-filled terrace. And yet the effect is not overpowering, particularly since she has avoided using rugs on the floor, preferring to let the old cream and black tiles take centre stage; in fact, the textiles add an air of femininity and comfort without making the space feel at all stuffy or overdressed.

Colour is her other tool. Although there are patterns in her textile collection, they are soft in tone and repetitive and geometric in design; the overall effect is of metres of soft, creamy fabric fading gently into the background. As for the use of paint, every structural element, from the chimney piece in the living room to the walls and ceiling both there and in the bedrooms – even the built-up sides of the staircase that descends to the lower floor – is painted either white or cream, with no attempt to add contrast or artificial excitement.

This deliberate simplicity, coupled with a feminine love and enjoyment of comfort and relaxation, is why the tiny house of Tita Bay is so successful. Who would not wish to step in off the street, shut the door and sink into one of the comfortable seats, at total peace with the world?

Ingenuity has been employed in this arrangement of shelf and hanging space – rough pieces of wood make up the shelf and hanging rail, while the hangers themselves have been made of driftwood and hooks (*this page*). A guest bedroom has been made in the attic, where the old beams dominate. All is pale and discreet, with the exception of the printed zebra rug (*opposite right*).

LYRICAL LEGACY

Carole Oulhen lives with her husband and family in a large, early 19th-century house in a village outside Avignon. Neither a mas nor a manoir, it is the type of house that can be seen in villages across France: solid, well-built and with a personality and a history very much its own.

Once a silkworm farm, the house was also, in the 19th century, the home of one of the poets who belonged to the Félibrige, a literary society whose members included Frédéric Mistral, Provence's most famous poet, and whose aim was to restore Occitan, *la langue d'Oc*, the old language of Provence.

Carole bought the house a few years ago and, although she appreciated its turn-of-the-century past, she wanted to adapt it for a modern family. Much structural work was needed, so by the time she came to what the majority would think the most interesting and amusing task – the furnishing and decorating of the rooms – her budget was limited.

In a large 19th-century village house, typical of many still to be found in every region of France, Carole Oulhen has restored the space to something of its former grandeur. In what was the only major structural alteration, a large kitchen and dining room has been made downstairs from what was once an outhouse that served as a garage. It is now a light, sunny room leading onto a broad terrace and from there to the garden. It has been decorated with taste and restraint. The colours are pale, the furniture carefully chosen and the details – the lined baskets beneath the sink mirrored by more baskets above the armoire – are in keeping with the overall style of the house (*this page and opposite*).

The large living room leads off the original entrance hall and is decorated, like the rest of the house, in calm, pale colours (*opposite*). The entrance hall, with its distinctive encaustic tiles, is a decorative feature in itself, with bands of painted colour in varying shades of stone (*this page*).

NATURAL LINENS AND MUSLINS PREDOMINATE, IN SOFT STONE SHADES OR TRADITIONAL PATTERNS SUCH AS TWO-TONED TOILES DE JOUY AND OLD FLORAL DESIGNS.

The arrangement of the downstairs rooms has a considered air of simplicity, echoing the architecture. The furniture, too, is neither all old nor all new; rather, each piece is chosen for its place in the finished picture. Pale linens and cottons are Carole's first choice, but she also likes the soft patterns of traditional toiles de Jouy (*opposite and this page*).

There is a feeling of almost austere simplicity all the bedrooms, both those on the ground and on the upper floor, where simple country furniture, pale, limpid tones and and neutral fabrics make for rooms that are both cool and restrained (*this page*). In a ground-floor room, an unlined curtain is dressed with gathered embroidery (*opposite*).

If anything, the house has benefited from this restraint. In every room, clean lines dominate; colours are gentle and furnishings are restrained. The impression is one of considered simplicity. For example, the hall is distinguished by fine 19th-century encaustic floor tiles, an integral part of the house that Carole has made into a prominent feature. To unify the space, she has paired the tiles with painted bands of colour in varying shades of stone on the walls. The hall makes a decorative statement that draws the eye towards the other rooms that lead off from it.

When the Oulhens bought the house, attached to it was a large outhouse, which the previous owners had used as a garage. They decided to knock through from the house into the outhouse to make one large space, now the large combined kitchen and dining room, which opens directly onto a terrace and the garden. It is a fine room, simply furnished and coloured, with clever touches such as baskets of differing sizes beneath the sink to hide unattractive essentials, and a large painted wooden armoire whose panels are filled with metal mosquito screening instead of glass.

The kitchen was the only room that was changed structurally. The configuration of the others remains the same. The living room is furnished as straightforwardly as the kitchen – a room of calm and peaceful colours based on Carole's favourite palette of stone. The same thinking applies to the bedrooms – three upstairs and one down.

The furniture incorporates a mixture of styles, with pieces chosen for their looks and charm rather than their rarity, and often painted in soft shades by Carole, who is an artist at heart. The textiles follow the same path – natural linens and muslins with accents of colour in the fabrics that have been used for cushions and throws, and traditional patterns such as two-toned toiles de Jouy and old floral designs.

Once a deep burgundy, the façade of the house is now a deep yellow ochre. Its garden owes much to early 19th-century design, with such charming features as old walls and fruit trees and a pond. The whole ensemble seems perfect – perhaps because Carole is a perfectionist. She is also someone who loves to restore old houses, so it would be no surprise if another sleeping house finds itself gently shaken awake by this restorer of both talent and taste.

FURNITURE PIECES WERE
CHOSEN FOR THEIR LOOKS AND
CHARM, AND OFTEN PAINTED IN
SOFT SHADES BY CAROLE, WHO
IS AN ARTIST AT HEART.

In the main bathroom, which is en suite, Carole has cleverly converted an antique washstand into an up-to-date, plumbed unit. The new ceramic basin, reminiscent of an antique china bowl, and the marble-topped, painted wooden stand both look as if they have always been there, and only the wall-hung taps/faucets give the secret away (*opposite*). In another bathroom, a similar effect of permanence has been achieved by the installation of a freestanding rolltop tub, a ladder-style rail and a crystal-drop chandelier (*this page*).

PRETTY AS A PICTURE

Diana Bauer and her husband found their 300-year-old farmhouse in Cotignac over 50 years ago, long before the current wave of Provence-lovers descended on the region. When they bought the house, it was tiny, and almost a ruin, not having been lived in for half a century.

Cotignac is one of the prettiest of the Haut-Var villages that perch high above the Mediterranean in a region dominated by vineyards and olive and chestnut groves. Like most other villages in the area, it is not a summer-only place. Go there in midwinter or spring and you will find open shops and cafés, competitive boules games in progress and a thriving weekly market.

When the Bauers bought the house, it consisted of just a downstairs living room with a sleeping alcove in the wall, an upstairs room for storing hay and an outbuilding used as a stable. Since it hadn't been lived in for a very long time, much had to be done to make it habitable without destroying the sense and charm of the original building. The first task was to deal with the structure – in particular, to renovate the stonework, which had deteriorated badly over the years. The next project was to add an internal staircase; at that time, the only way to reach the upper rooms was by external stone steps. To retain the atmosphere of the original building, the Bauers made the ground floor into a living space and kitchen, and converted the old hay loft into three bedrooms, two large and one small, and a bathroom.

TO RETAIN THE ATMOSPHERE OF THE
ORIGINAL BUILDING, THE GROUND FLOOR WAS
MADE INTO A LIVING SPACE AND KITCHEN.

The kitchen is a comfortable and familiar
room. It features pine cupboards and
traditional Provençal-print curtains, which,
in time-honoured fashion, are used to hide
all the utilitarian pots and pans beneath
the work surfaces (*above and right*).

A sleeping alcove in the living room has become a real hideaway – ideal for relaxing close to the fire on a winter's evening, and equally convenient as an extra bed space (*left*). In keeping with the rest of the house, the main bedroom is, above all, comfortable. Two chairs – one a traditional rocking chair, the other an old French country chair – are both conducive to relaxation (*opposite*).

The sleeping alcove in the downstairs room was made into a whitewashed, cushion-piled bed to be used day and night. In the kitchen, too, all has been done with the utmost simplicity. There are pine doors under the worktops and a large pine cupboard used as a larder. Upstairs bedrooms have old terracotta floors, simple furniture, rag rugs and American patchwork quilts, which work very well in these light-filled rooms.

In the garden, several large pieces of stone topped with a rough-hewn slab were used to make a table in front of a stone bench that protrudes from the walls of the house; elsewhere, a low wall doubles as a bench. French windows curve round the house, making inside and out appear as one. The original outside staircase is flanked with pots of geraniums and lavender, and vines and wisteria climb over the terrace. It is unpretentious and charming and completely of Provence.

THERE WAS ORIGINALLY JUST A DOWNSTAIRS LIVING ROOM WITH A SLEEPING ALCOVE IN THE WALL, AN UPSTAIRS ROOM FOR STORING HAY AND AN OUTBUILDING USED AS A STABLE.

Architecture has been put to good use in another part of the garden, where a low wall doubles as a bench in front of a table. Set underneath a fig tree, the scene is illuminated by an appropriate flowerpot light (*opposite*). The pleasure of summer in Provence is that, for so many months of the year, life takes place outside in the garden or on the terrace; sunny living is about moving seamlessly from inside to outside through French windows and open doors, just like this cat (*this page*).

The Château de Gignac was brought back to life by the Jouberts, and every space, both outside and in, has been renovated and restored in the most sympathetic way. In the enormous entrance hall, for example, Michelle was careful not to over-decorate or over-furnish. On one side of the hall is a carved, painted and gilded console table crowned with a distinguished but simple period mirror. On the other side of the hall, beneath the staircase, is a traditional Provençal three-seated bench known as a *radassié*. Other than a pair of tall candlesticks, the space is empty – all the better to appreciate the pattern of the worn stone floor and the sweep of the elegant staircase (*opposite and below*).

GLORY RESTORED

After she and her late husband bought the Château de Gignac in 1989, Michelle Joubert took on the task of returning it to the glory it might have enjoyed had not the hand of history intervened; for many years, she worked on the house using only old materials and recreated every room to perfection.

France's size and its turbulent past mean that, particularly in the South, visual reminders of its history are often seen. There is still evidence of the destruction wrought by the 16th-century Wars of Religion, and people tend to talk about the years of the French Revolution as if they had only just taken place.

Take the troubled and, until modern times, tragic story of the Château de Gignac, for example. At the place on which the present château stands there was once a medieval castle. Like many other buildings in the area, this was destroyed during the Wars of Religion. By the 18th century, a new château was under construction on the site, built by an old Provençal family, the de Thomas, but just before its completion, the events set in train by the French Revolution caused the Marquis de Thomas to flee, never to return, and the château, like so many others, fell into disrepair.

It remained in that state until the end of the 1980s, when it was bought by Michelle Joubert and her late husband François.

Many rural châteaux are less like castles than large, sometimes fortified, manor houses; they are often the centre of an agricultural smallholding, and the hub of a community. Looking at the Château de Gignac today, you can see how, under Michelle's sensitive direction, such a house would have developed had it been constantly inhabited since the 18th century. Yet there was literally nothing there when the Jouberts bought it; all had to be found and bought – as Michelle says, 'everything, piece by piece' – at auction, in antique shops, at brocantes and, of course, in the market of L'Isle-sur-la-Sorgue. Even the bathrooms have been carefully designed to look as though they might have been added at the end of the 19th century.

Although there is this sense of age, and although Michelle consistently used old materials, furniture and furnishings, and even though both architecture and decoration consistently refer to the past, the house looks neither old-fashioned nor preserved in amber; indeed, one of its abiding triumphs is that it looks so of the moment – but a moment achieved with old pieces. In every room, the old is placed in such a way that it looks completely modern, and things that are intrinsically old – textiles, decorative objects and so on – are arranged in a subtle manner. The hall, a dramatic space in any large house, has few pieces of furniture: a flamboyant console, a large wall-hung mirror and, on the floor, an oversized candlestick.

The age of the stonework and tiles on this outside terrace, as well as the original sturdy painted shutters, add to the charm and tranquillity of this sitting area, enveloped as it is in greenery (*right*).

In part of what was once the scullery, Michelle put together a large collection of Provençal pottery – all practical, working pieces that would have been used as often 200 years ago as they are today. The various pieces are all displayed and stored in rows and piles, much as they would originally have been, and their glazes, set against a backdrop of old terracotta and stone, are seen to antique advantage (*this page and opposite*).

In the curve of the stairwell sits a traditional Provençal *radassié*, a wood-backed banquette. The relative sparseness of the room serves to emphasize both the sweeping staircase itself and the dramatic cobbled floor, worn in places and evocative of times past.

The same feeling continues throughout the house: the kitchen is a combination of the romantic – an old refectory table and a worn, well-used butcher's block – and the practical, represented by a new cooking range, designed in traditional style and set into the old hearth. The main reception rooms are simply but elegantly furnished with moulded plaster panels, carefully chosen pieces of furniture and generously full curtains that brush the floor.

The eight bedrooms are reassuringly old-fashioned and yet not fussy; as in the downstairs rooms, relatively little furniture is used in each room, with only the odd decorative piece. The wall colourings are used to add extra decoration, all silvery and soft: light grey, eggshell blue and pale rose, sometimes with delicate plaster moulding, and woodwork highlighted in soft French whites.

The bathroom fixtures, traditional in design, are cleverly combined with freestanding pieces of furniture, some originally made to hold washbowls and ewers. Michelle deliberately decorated the bathrooms with pictures, mirrors and objects more often seen in grander surroundings.

Outside, the gardens and terraces are planted in traditional and Provençal style, with a swimming pool designed in the shape of a long, classical, stone-edged canal. The 18th-century Marquis de Thomas would doubtless have much appreciated the 21st-century Château de Gignac.

In a bed alcove, the walls are a very pale duck-egg blue, contrasting with, and yet complementing, the soft grey of the rest of the room. The stucco has been left unrestored, and the polished terracotta tiles throw the whole scheme into relief (*above*). In an upper hall, pale grey walls are emphasized by a deeper dove grey in the alcoves and on the door panels. The original plaster moulding has been restored and painted a soft creamy-white, offsetting the grey and white marble floor tiles (*opposite*).

THE WALL COLOURINGS
ARE USED TO ADD EXTRA
DECORATION, ALL SILVERY AND
SOFT: LIGHT GREY, EGGSHELL
BLUE AND PALE ROSE,
SOMETIMES CONTRASTING WITH
DELICATE PLASTER MOULDING,
AND WOODWORK HIGHLIGHTED
IN SOFT FRENCH WHITES.

Bedroom colours are typically soft and 18th century in feel. These rooms are enlivened with a single piece of decorative drama. In one bedroom, an antique mirror and painting have been set into a painted and gilded frame (*opposite*). A serpentine commode with marble top is painted in a traditional soft blue (*above*). The other bedroom has plain terracotta flooring, trompe l'oeil dado panelling and an extravagant flourish in the form of a carved and gilded piece of religious ornament (*right*).

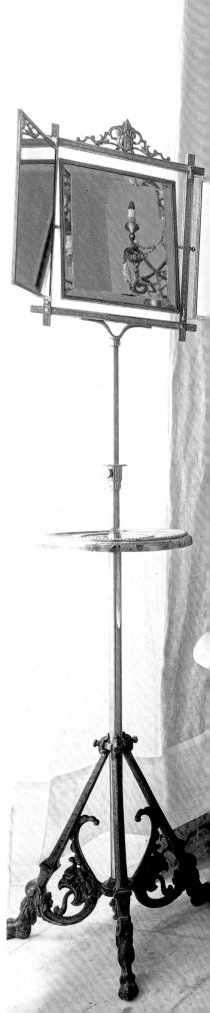

The simply arranged bathrooms are given an air of permanence by a combination of old furniture and new plumbing. In one room, a long piece of furniture, possibly the base of an old dresser/hutch, has been converted into a modern basin unit, complete with more than enough storage space for towels and bathroom pieces (*above*). Although the tubs and basins are of traditional design, it is the charm of the accompanying furnishings that brings these rooms to life. Seen here are an 18th-century landscape above a curtained vanity and an exuberant gilded circular mirror hanging over a bathtub (*left and right*).

INDEX

Page numbers in *italic* refer to the illustrations

PICTURE CREDITS

All photography by Christopher Drake except where stated.
Ph = photographer.

Front cover: Annie-Camille Kuentzmann-Levet's house in Yvelines; Back cover: Diana Bauer's house near Cotignac, styling by Enrica Stabile; 1 ph. Jan Baldwin/Architecture in miniature www.petergabrielse.com; 2 ph. Jan Baldwin/The Normandy home of Fiona Atkins of Town House, Spitalfields; 3 ph. Peter Cassidy; 4 left ph. Simon Brown; 4 centre ph. Peter Cassidy; 4 right ph. Simon Brown; 5 ph. Jan Baldwin/The house of Bert and Julia Huizenga, south of Toulouse at the foothills of the Pyrenees; 6 Florence and Pierre Pallardy, Domaine de la Baronnie, Saint Martin de Ré; 7 ph. Martin Brigdale; 9 Enrica Stabile's house in Le Thor, Provence; 10–11 ph. Jan Baldwin/The house of Bert and Julia Huizenga, south of Toulouse at the foothills of the Pyrenees; 12–13 ph. Jan Baldwin/ The home of Françoise Piccino www.la-cabane-de-jeanne.com; 14 left ph. Simon Brown; 14 centre ph. Martin Brigdale; 14 right Owners of La Cour Beaudeval Antiquities, Mireille and Jean Claude Lothon's house in Faverolles; 15 ph. Jan Baldwin/The home of Sara Giunta and Jean-Luc Charrier of La Maison de Charrier in Valbonne; 16 Alain and Catherine Brunel's hotel, La Maison Douce, Saint Martin de Ré; 17 Annie-Camille Kuentzmann-Levet's house in Yvelines; 18 Annie-Camille Kuentzmann-Levet's house in Yvelines; 19 above Owners of La Cour Beaudeval Antiquities, Mireille and Jean Claude Lothon's house in Faverolles; 19 below The home of Nicole Albert, owner of House La France, which is available for rental www.houselafrance.com; 20 above Julie Prisca's house in Normandy; 20 below Ph. Jan Baldwin/The house of Bert and Julia Huizenga, south of Toulouse at the foothills of the Pyrenees; 21 Owners of La Cour Beaudeval Antiquities, Mireille and Jean Claude Lothon's house in Faverolles; 22 ph. Jan Baldwin; 23 ph. Jan Baldwin/The late Giorgio and Irene Silvagni's house in Provence; 24 left ph. Jan Baldwin/The house of Bert and Julia Huizenga, south of Toulouse at the foothills of the Pyrenees; 24 centre ph. Simon Brown; 24 right ph. Simon Brown; 25 ph. Jan Baldwin; 26 ph. Jan Baldwin/The house of Bert and Julia Huizenga, south of Toulouse at the foothills of the Pyrenees; 27 ph. Jan Baldwin/The home of Sara Giunta and Jean-Luc Charrier of La Maison de Charrier in Valbonne; 28–29 La Bastide de Marie, Ménerbes www.labastidedemarie.com; 30 ph. Jan Baldwin/The late Giorgio and Irene Silvagni's house in Provence; 31 ph. Jan Baldwin/The Normandy home of Fiona Atkins of Town House, Spitalfields; 32 Enrica Stabile's house in Le Thor, Provence; 33 above ph. Jan Baldwin/Home of the French designer Catherine-Hélène Frei www.cathfrei.com; 33 below left Annie Camille Kuentzmann-Levet's house in Yvelines; 33 below right ph. Jan Baldwin/The home of the French designer Catherine-Hélène Frei www.cathfrei.com; 34 Interior designer Carole Ouhlen; 35 A country house near Mougins, Provence; 36 La Bastide de Marie, Ménerbes www.labastidedemarie.com; 37 Owners of La Cour Beaudeval Antiquities, Mireille and Jean Claude Lothon's house in Faverolles; 38 above Annie-Camille Kuentzmann-Levet's house in Yvelines; 38 below Alain and Catherine Brunel's hotel, La Maison Douce, Saint Martin de Ré; 39 Anna Bonde and artist Arne Tengblad's home in the Luberon Valley, Provence; 40–41 Annie-Camille Kuentzmann-Levet's house in Yvelines; 42 left ph. Claire Richardson/ The home of Jean-Louis Fages and Matthieu Ober in Nimes; 42 centre Owners of La Cour Beaudeval Antiquities, Mireille and Jean Claude Lothon's house in Faverolles; 42 right ph. Simon Brown; 43 A country house near Mougins, Provence; 44 Owners of La Cour Beaudeval Antiquities, Mireille and Jean Claude Lothon's house in Faverolles; 45 above Monique Davidson's family home in Normandy; 45 below Owners of La Cour Beaudeval Antiquities, Mireille and Jean Claude Lothon's house in Faverolles; 46 above left and below Owner Monique Davidson's family home in Normandy 46 above right Florence and Pierre Pallardy, Domaine de la Baronnie, Saint Martin de Ré; 47 Anna Bonde and artist Arne Tengblad's home in the Luberon Valley, Provence; 48 above Anna Bonde and artist Arne Tengblad's home in the Luberon Valley, Provence; 48 below Owners of La Cour Beaudeval Antiquities, Mireille and Jean Claude Lothon's house in Faverolles; 49 Annie-Camille Kuentzmann-Levet's house in Yvelines; 50 left ph. Christopher Drake; 50 centre ph. Jan Baldwin/The home of Ilse van der Meerakker owner of www.maisonvivreplus.nl; 50 right ph. Martin Brigdale; 51 ph. Simon Brown; 52 above Annie-Camille Kuentzmann-Levet's house in Yvelines; 52 below La Bastide de Marie, Ménerbes www.labastidedemarie.com; 53 above Julie Prisca's house in Normandy; 53 below left Owners of La Cour Beaudeval Antiquities, Mireille and Jean Claude Lothon's house in Faverolles; 53 below right A country house near Mougins, Provence; 54 above left and right ph. Simon Brown; 54 below The Chateau de Gignac, Michelle Joubert's former home in Provence; 55 ph. Jan Baldwin/ Home of the French designer Catherine-Hélène Frei www.cathfrei.com; 56 The Chateau de Gignac, Michelle Joubert's former home in Provence; 57 above The Chateau de Gignac, Michelle Joubert's former home in Provence; 57 below La Bastide de Marie, Ménerbes www.labastidedemarie.com; 58–59 ph. Jan Baldwin/The late Giorgio and Irene Silvagni's house in Provence; 60–71 Pavilion de Levant, gatehouse on the property of Pavilion de Victoire, Verneques, France, designed by Kenyon Kramer and Jean-Louis Raynaud; 72–81 Owners of French Country Living, the Hill family's home on the Cote D'Azur; 82–93 The home of the late Maurizo Epifani, owner of l'Oro dei Farlocchi; 94–105 décoratrice Nelly Guyot's home; 106–115 Enrica Stabile's house in Le Thor, Provence;116–127 Villa Marie, Ramatuelle, St Tropez; 128–137 A family home near Aix-en-Provence with interior design by Daisy Simon; 138–149 The late Giorgio and Irene Silvagni's house in Provence; 150–157 Tita Bay's village house in Ramatuelle; 158–167 interior designer Carole Ouhlen; 168–175 Diana Bauer's house near Cotignac, styling by Enrica Stabile; 176–187 The Chateau de Gignac, Michelle Joubert's former home in Provence; 190 ph. Jan Baldwin/ The late Giorgio and Irene Silvagni's house in Provence; 192 ph. Jan Baldwin/The house of Bert and Julia Huizenga, south of Toulouse at the foothills of the Pyrenees; Endpapers ph. Peter Cassidy.

ACKNOWLEDGEMENTS

Writing and editing this book reminded me yet again of just how tantalisingly beautiful and rich France is. Round every corner and through every doorway there is the promise of something new to discover and delight, some examples of which we have tried to show in the pages of Summers in France.

I would very much like to thank the team at Ryland Peters & Small: Annabel Morgan, Leslie Harrington, Megan Smith, Patricia Harrington and Jess Walton, who really were a team, helping me all the way through the process. I'd especially like to thank my editor, Sophie Devlin, for her understanding and help with my total lack of computer savvy, which would have tried the patience of a saint, never mind a book editor!

And of course, there would be no chronicle of any of these decorative delights were it not for the generosity of all the talented and creative owners who allowed their houses to be photographed in the first place, and who were willing to explain just how they attained their particular goals. I would like to thank them all very much indeed.

Caroline Clifton-Mogg